Cambridge Latin Course
Unit I
Teacher's Handbook

Cambridge Latin Course
Unit I
Teacher's Handbook

Cambridge · at the University Press 1971

Published by the Syndics of the Cambridge University Press
Bentley House, 200 Euston Road, London N.W.1
American Branch: 32 East 57th Street, New York, N.Y.10022

© Cambridge University Press 1971

Library of Congress Catalogue Card Number: 72–132282

ISBN: 0 521 07902 0

Printed in Great Britain
at the University Printing House, Cambridge
(Brooke Crutchley, University Printer)

Contents

Preface

In 1966 the Cambridge School Classics Project began work on a two-fold brief: first to develop new materials and techniques for teaching Latin to G.C.E. 'O' level; and second to devise a non-linguistic Foundation Course in Classical Studies. This was a curriculum development project sponsored jointly by the Faculty Board of Classics and the Education Syndicate of Cambridge University, and its existence was made possible by the generosity of the Trustees of the Nuffield Foundation and of the Schools Council, who have borne jointly the costs of the Project.

The Cambridge Latin Course is one of the results of the Project's work during the past four years; and it is hoped that it will make a contribution to the continuous process of re-appraising the role of Classics within the school curriculum. Before publication, extensive trials of the materials in experimental form were conducted in the classrooms of ninety-six schools in Great Britain. A great debt is owed to the teachers and pupils who participated in this programme and whose constructive criticisms have contributed so much to the making of the Course.

We also wish to record our gratitude to the members of the Project's Advisory Panel, representing University Departments of Classics, University Departments of Education and teachers of Classics in schools; the Faculty Board of Classics for its generosity in making a grant of £500 towards the cost of photographic work; the Syndics of the Cambridge University Press for much practical assistance; the Director of the Naples Museum for permission to photograph the sites at Pompeii and Herculaneum and exhibits in the museum itself; the members of the Project Committee who, in spite of countless other calls on their time, have given themselves so generously to our needs; and all those scholars, too numerous to mention here by name, who have allowed us to consult them so frequently. Their advice and encouragement have been invaluable. We hope that we have been able to make effective use of their help, but responsibility for the imperfections that remain lies entirely with the Project team.

D. C. CHANDLER	J. A. JONES
M. ST J. FORREST	D. J. MORTON
C. GREIG	E. P. STORY
R. M. GRIFFIN	

Cambridge 1970

Introduction

This Latin course has two main objectives. The first is to teach comprehension of the Latin language for reading purposes. The second is to develop from the outset an understanding of the content, style and values of Roman civilisation, with particular reference to the first century A.D. The course presents the language not as an end in itself, nor as an instrument of general mental training, but rather as a means of gaining access to a literature and the culture from which it springs. The study of that literature is one, though by no means the only one, of the intellectual experiences which contribute to the growth of civilised thought and sensitivity; and it is for this reason, more than for any other, that it has a part to play in the educational process. To fulfil this purpose, however, the teacher of Latin must see the objective clearly and must pursue it with means that are effective and reasonably economical of time.

The teaching of Latin in schools has too often been divorced, for want of time, from the study of the Roman world, with the result that when pupils begin to read original authors their grasp of the background is inadequate for a proper understanding of what they read. We have, therefore, tried to integrate language and culture very closely from the beginning of the course. The reading material is based upon actual Roman situations and frequently uses historical characters.

Another problem that commonly occurs in Latin teaching is the gap between the Latin of the course books which cater for the early stages and the Latin of the original texts which are begun in the third or fourth year of the course. Pupils often find the transition difficult; both interest and momentum can easily decline at this point. To some extent the difficulty is inherent in the nature of the Latin they are learning to read, for it is not the language of daily conversation or newspapers; it is the language of a sophisticated literature. This, however, is not the sole cause of the difficulty. In our view the problem also derives from certain characteristics of conventional methods of teaching. For example, it is customary to try to impart several linguistic skills more or less simultaneously, namely formal analysis of grammar, composition and reading. This practice, on which most current course books are based, assumes that the first two of these skills contribute materially to the acquisition of the third and are even indispensable to it. The assumption is at least questionable. Another common characteristic of Latin teaching is the tendency to stress the forms of words, particularly their inflexional aspects, rather than the shape or pattern of the sentence. Yet it is experience of sentences, where form and function are encountered together, that is fundamental to the successful development of reading competence. In order to help pupils to approach literary Latin with more confidence and success, this course has modified the perspective of the language that is usually presented and has dispensed with teaching practices that do not seem to us to be directly or immediately relevant.

A further central question is that of interest. Some pupils, though probably only a minority, find sufficient interest and motivation in the study of the language itself, but the majority hope to find interest in what the texts say. Too often, in the early stages, they are disappointed; and they give up the subject without achieving any real insight into its social or literary content. The picture of the Roman world presented to them frequently lacks coherence or human credibility; it is often excessively military or vaguely historical. It fails to present a picture of a living society. We hope that by offering the pupil narrative and dramatic stories which are culturally valid and which attempt to depict Roman life in realistic detail this course may help to satisfy his reasonable expectations. If the pupil's interest is engaged by the content of the language, his chances of mastering the language itself will be greatly improved.

In many schools the objectives of reading skill and study of Roman culture will have to be pursued within a smaller allowance of time than is sometimes available today. A number of schools still offer a five-year course to 'O' level, starting at the age of eleven. Many, perhaps still the majority, offer a four-year course from the age of twelve, but an increasing number will restrict their course to three years or even to two. In these circumstances it becomes even more essential to define one's aims as precisely as possible and to devise methods that are strictly relevant. One important effect of the later starting age, with the consequent removal of Latin from the first and second year of the secondary curriculum, has been to create more scope for the non-linguistic Classical Foundation courses. These are not an entirely new feature of classical teaching, but interest in them has grown rapidly in recent years. Many teachers have experimented with their own syllabuses and materials, and the supply of suitable books has steadily improved in quantity and quality. The Cambridge Project has strongly recommended that advantage be taken of this opportunity and has developed its own materials for a non-linguistic Foundation Course. When classroom trials and revision have been completed, it will be published by the Cambridge University Press. Courses of this kind are designed particularly for the needs of mixed ability classes in comprehensive schools, but also have a place in the selective school. They are not intended to cater only for those pupils who will later begin to learn a classical language, Latin or Greek; their purpose is to bring the classical world into the field of general education and to make it accessible, through the medium of English, to pupils in the whole range of ability. Experience has already demonstrated that they have the further value of stimulating some pupils to ask for a chance to learn the Latin or Greek language.

There are other and more fundamental reasons for considering the possibility of change, change both in the content of the Latin course and in the methods of teaching it. During the past twenty years research in theoretical linguistics has made important advances. These are in no sense final—indeed many questions, such as how children actually acquire language, are only at an exploratory stage— but nevertheless certain concepts have been worked out sufficiently to justify their application to Latin teaching. Perhaps the most significant idea has been that the whole sentence rather than the individual word is the primary unit of meaning.

The sentence conveys the essential message that the hearer or reader must arrive at, but it is not a simple aggregation of smaller units, namely words, strung together in an order that may be flexible or fairly rigid. The sentence has a structure, often complex, through which the interrelationship of words and groups of words is expressed. This structure is crucial for meaning. Words in themselves yield important lexical information by distinguishing, for example, between 'houses' and 'ships', 'running' and 'walking', 'fear' and 'joy';

nevertheless it is the way in which they are brought together and the rules governing their association that make the difference between an arbitrary list and a meaningful utterance. One of the tasks of modern theoretical linguistics has been to explore these structural patterns more intensively and deeply than traditional grammars have been able to do. The outcome of this work has not been, as some have supposed, the abandonment of the familiar categories of traditional grammar, for they are part of the truth about language and certainly about Latin. But there has emerged a new emphasis on the role of word-groups and the way in which they combine into successively larger units. A language may or may not be heavily inflected, but it always has syntactic structure. Inflexion and word order are seen more as sub-systems within this essential structural characteristic. Hence the primary task involved in learning a second language is to make it possible for the learner to recognise the sentence and phrase structures correctly. The observation of inflexional variables and word order has of course a part to play in the process, but is not sufficient in itself.

The development of insight and ready recognition of the structures will probably be facilitated rather by presenting the learner from the outset with complete sentences, carefully selected and designed, than by the more usual procedure which begins with analysis at word-level and then tries to jump from there to understanding at sentence-level. The difficulty of this latter procedure is familiar in the class-room. The pupil is told to study carefully the endings of the words and is trained to describe them by declension, conjugation and other categories, the implication being that when he can account for words in this way he will also be able to grasp the meaning of the sentence as a whole. When he fails, as frequently happens, we try to help him further by instructing him to pick out the subject, the verb, the object and so on until the sentence has been re-arranged into some English order. There is an inherent disadvantage in this practice: it tends to convey the idea that Latin structure is at best obscure and cannot be comprehended until English word order has been imposed on it. Thus in trying to help the pupil to make the progression from the description of words to an understanding of the sentence we may considerably undermine his confidence in Latin as a language. Able pupils gradually learn to handle these different levels successfully;

the less able remain confused. It is tempting to think that the answer to the difficulty lies in more efficient drilling of formal Latin grammar or even in more study of English grammar. Neither seems to us to provide the best solution. We have approached the problem from the other end by trying to apply structural rules to the design of the learning materials, so as to provide the pupil with intensive practice of phrase and sentence structures, and only a minimum of formal information about the inflexional system. In this way, it is hoped that he will learn the crucial lesson of structure more successfully and acquire a truer perspective of the role of inflexion. For a fuller discussion of the linguistic basis the reader is referred to Appendix A at the end of this book.

The age at which pupils begin Latin is very variable, but the general introduction of comprehensive schools is likely to mean that it will in future be later than it used to be. It is doubtful whether any particular age in the usual range from ten to fourteen can claim to have great advantages over any other. Early starters advance more slowly, the later more quickly. But what is sometimes overlooked by those who make curriculum decisions is that language competence requires practice and experience; the foundations need time to become firm. Without sufficient time neither efficiency nor good pace can be achieved. Two or three periods a week are not enough; four should be the minimum.

The pupil's material is divided into 'stages', each containing one or two new linguistic advances, together with consolidation of previous advances. The stages take the form of separate pamphlets, each numbered and with its own title indicating the main theme of the stage. The stages themselves are grouped into a total of five units of varying length. Unit I consists of Stages 1–12. The time required to complete any one stage varies and the teacher will have to find the right balance of thoroughness and good pace according to the needs of the class and the time available. Generally, Units I and II will be completed in the first year, and the longer and more difficult Unit III will occupy the second year. In the case of a three-year 'O' level course this rate of progress would be stepped up and Units I–III completed in four terms, with Units IV and V taking a further two terms. For younger pupils starting at eleven this pace would be considerably reduced.

Units I, II and III consist of made-up Latin prose. Units IV and V effect the transition to original Latin. They include verse selected from Catullus, Martial, Ovid and Virgil and prose from Pliny and Tacitus. The prose is heavily adapted initially and advances toward largely unchanged original Latin.

An 'O' level syllabus and examination specially designed for this course is now offered by the Southern Universities Joint Board, and may be adopted by any school, on application to the Board which the school normally uses. The syllabus is the Cambridge Project 'O' level Latin Syllabus. Candidates who take this examination will, if they are successful, receive the Certificate of the Board through which the application was made. Further information may be obtained from the Secretary, Southern Universities Joint Board, Cotham Road, Bristol BS6 6DD.

Finally, we hope that this book will prove useful to both young and experienced teachers. The suggestions made in the following chapters are not intended to be rigid prescriptions; teachers will wish to adjust their methods to suit the needs of their pupils as they see them. The principles described here are those on which this particular course was constructed and which, during an extensive programme of class-room trials, were found by most teachers and pupils to be effective. In so far as they stimulate efficient learning and genuine interest, it is hoped that they will contribute to the future well-being of Latin as a respected component of humane education.

1 The Pupil's Material

The pamphlets

The format of the pupil's material differs from that of the usual coursebook. It consists of a series of pamphlets; each pamphlet is called a stage, and the stages are grouped into units. Unit I has twelve stages of reading material and a vocabulary pamphlet.

Why pamphlets?

The material has been constructed in this way in order to allow teachers to present each stage to the class when it is needed and not before. This system was adopted during the extensive pre-publication trials and proved to be practicable and popular with teachers and pupils alike. It gives to each stage the maximum freshness of impact. Pupils are not daunted by the sight of all the ground to be covered in the future, but see a steady accumulation of work completed. The pupil's wallet will hold one unit of pamphlets. When full it should be emptied and the unit returned to the stock cupboard. The wallet is used again for the next unit.

Arrangement of the stage

Most stages begin with several pages on which a new feature of the language is presented prominently by means of *model sentences* or, in later stages, short paragraphs, accompanied by line drawings. At the end of the sentences there usually follows a short *note about the language*, whenever some formal comment is thought to be required. Fuller notes are provided for the teacher's use in the Stage Commentaries of this Handbook (pp. 45–112).

The model sentences and language note are followed by several *narrative or dramatic passages* in which the new and old linguistic features are rehearsed. These passages are the central core of each stage. They increase in length and complexity as the course advances, but the gradient has been carefully controlled. Many of the stories will fit conveniently into one lesson; others will require longer. Beneath each passage are listed new words and phrases; they are given in the form in which they occur in the story and are glossed in the sense required by the context. Long vowels are marked by macrons in these lists, but not in the text of the stories.

Next come the *manipulation exercises*. In the early stages they practise the new linguistic features, but soon they concentrate upon important features taught in preceding stages and are intended to serve mainly as consolidation. Thus the exercises are largely, though not exclusively, retrospective in purpose. It is important to note that the manipulation is conducted in Latin and by translation from Latin. There are no exercises that require translation from English into Latin. Many take the form of sentence completion by the selection of a word or phrase from a given pool. In some stages there are also additional passages to be read and translated or discussed.

The final section of a stage consists of *paralinguistic material*. This term is used to denote both written and visual material which aids the exploration of cultural issues arising from the written passages. This section, written in English, tries to do more than simply impart information; it seeks to give a picture of a living society and to raise questions of behaviour, attitudes and tastes. It is our view that the larger issues should be handled in the classroom and at a level of maturity corresponding to pupils' capacity and interest. We regard it as essential that they should be encouraged to learn something of the rhythm of daily life, the fabric of social relationships, the atmosphere of business and politics, styles of recreation and leisure, and above all something of the stock of ideas which in the hands of creative writers emerged as literature. To delay this until pupils actually begin to read original authors is to delay too long. The process should start from the beginning of the course. Clearly in the circumstances of a short course the paralinguistic material in the pamphlets and the showing and discussing of slides cannot be given a large proportion of class time; but its importance is such that if it is omitted altogether or handled only rarely, the course as a whole will be seriously impoverished.

2 The Role of the Teacher

The course has been designed primarily for pupils who are between eleven and thirteen years of age when they begin, and is intended to be used in a normal teaching situation where a group of pupils, up to about thirty in number, is being taught by a qualified teacher. It has not been designed specifically for beginners over the age of sixteen or for those who require materials for self-instruction. Evidence, however, suggests that the course can be used quite successfully in a variety of special circumstances.

The use of slides and tapes on a regular basis will require the teacher to be familiar with the way to operate a standard slide projector and tape-recorder and to know how to use these to good effect. Some detailed suggestions are made in Chapters 5 and 6. It should, however, be emphasised that this is not a course in which responsibility for guiding pupils' learning has been transferred largely from the teacher to some other agency of control. Neither the pamphlets nor the technical aids will of themselves teach pupils to read Latin. The part to be played by the teacher in this process will be central.

The aim of the varied techniques recommended here is to enable the pamphlets to have the optimum effect and to help the pupil to respond to the material in an active and personal way. Sometimes the teacher's role will be central in the sense that he will be actively and directly presenting the material to the class; he will be taking the initiative in bringing it to life. At other times, his role will be more oblique and less prominent. This will be so when, having set up a learning situation, he lets the class, either individually or in groups, get to work, while he circulates to give help where it is needed.

The stages are constructed on the assumption that at the beginning of each fresh advance into the language there will be a controlled dialogue between teacher and class. No attempt has been made in the pupil's text to answer all the questions that may or are likely to occur, nor are there numerous explanations to be read and memorised. These omissions, which may at first seem surprising, reflect our view that the answers will be much more effective if given directly by the teacher in reply to specific questions raised in a particular context. The problems of talking about language to pupils are discussed more fully in Appendix A; and it will be seen that we strongly discourage much discussion of this kind. But the point stressed here is that the teacher plays the key role in gauging the linguistic needs of pupils and satisfying them appropriately as the need emerges.

It is also hoped that the teacher will often turn the dialogue away from himself and allow pupils to read on their own. During the classroom trials of the course many teachers responded to the Project's invitation to experiment with group reading methods, a technique which has not generally been exploited in the Latin lesson in the past. For this purpose the class is divided into pairs or into groups of three, four or five pupils. They tackle a piece of Latin together, checking and assisting each other. The teacher moves round the groups and becomes a member of each in turn. His role is to help resolve any difficulties that have proved too great for the group by itself, to assess the accuracy of the reading, to test individuals and to put questions that stimulate thought about the context of the passage.

Experience suggests that this technique, whether used much or about once a week, helps to increase the pace of reading and enhances motivation. More details about it are given in the chapter on teaching methods. It is a good example of moving the teaching role from a central to an oblique position, so that pupils may be given more scope for their own initiative and may work at their own speed. Indeed, in classes that contain a fairly wide spectrum of ability, it may prove desirable to use group methods for a substantial part of the time.

3 Teaching Methods

Because this Course dispenses with some of the aims of other Latin courses, it has been necessary to modify classroom techniques quite extensively and to devise new ones more conducive to reading skill. In this chapter the main methods that have been found to be helpful and the principles underlying them are considered.

Model sentences

Principles

(1) These sentences, standing at the beginning of each stage, introduce linguistic advances. Sometimes they make a morphological point, such as the forms of the plural in Stage 5 or of the imperfect and perfect tenses in Stage 6; sometimes they introduce a new sentence pattern such as 'amicus Caecilium salutat' in Stage 2 or 'mercator feminis togas ostendit' in Stage 9.

(2) The linguistic advance is shown in a simple sentence accompanied by an illustration that points to the general sense-area of that sentence. The illustration not only makes the point that language is a part of human behaviour but also gives some information about the world in which Latin was used. The illustrations also help pupils to envisage more clearly the character and role of some of the people they meet in the stories.

(3) The model sentences thus aim at providing an easy initial experience of the new feature of language. They are intended to be read and understood. They are not intended to be used as the basis of a full discussion about that feature; but where some generalisations may usefully be made the short note at the end of the sentences indicates the way this should be done. It will be found that pupils remember many of these sentences accurately and can recall where they first occurred.

(4) Pupils are not expected to have achieved a completely accurate grasp of the new feature by the end of the model sentences. This grasp develops gradually through subsequent experience.

Teaching method

(1) The first step is to establish quickly the situation depicted in the sentences. This may often be done by discussing the picture on the outside cover of the pamphlet. This step should be very brief. Resist the temptation to expand the theme at this point.

(2) The teacher will normally guide the class through the initial exploration of the model sentences. Read aloud the first sentence or group of sentences in Latin. Give pupils a few moments to make their own attempts to understand. Then ask questions in English, using the picture as a guide. The technique of asking questions in this situation calls for a little thought and care. The old formula 'find the subject, find the verb' will not be appropriate. Couch the questions in concrete terms. For example:

Quintus in horto sedet.
Q. Who is in the picture?
A. Quintus.
Q. Good. Is Quintus standing or walking or sitting?
A. Sitting.
Q. Where?
A. In the garden.
Q. So what does the whole sentence mean?
A. Quintus is sitting in the garden.

It is of the utmost importance that *no comment* about the new feature should be given in advance. The pupils are to *discover the sense of it* for themselves aided by the context which generally gives powerful clues. The teacher's contribution is limited to concrete questions, in so far as these are necessary to elicit the meaning, and to supplying vocabulary information where needed. Experience has shown that many, if not all, pupils grasp the main point at the first or second example.

(3) When the sentence has been understood and expressed in English, pass straight on to the next sentence. Postpone discussion about the feature until all the sentences have been read.

(4) Keep up the pace. The teacher's reading of the Latin should be slow enough to be clear and distinct, but the movement from item to item and the transition from teacher to class and back again should be brisk.

(5) When working through the sentences, take the opportunity of exploring with the class some of the cultural features in the drawings. It may be helpful to come back to them later for further, more detailed discussion.

(6) After the first reading, *either* re-read with the assistance of the tape-recording *or* set the class to re-read individually or in pairs. At this point, when the meaning of the sentences has been understood, pupils should read the Latin aloud.

(7) The language note may now be used. The Project's approach to this aspect of language learning has been to limit comment strictly and keep terminology to a minimum. In this respect the Project's view of what is desirable stands in marked contrast to previous practice. The reasons for preferring this approach are set out in Appendix A, but the essential point is that comparison of the Latin with its English equivalent or equivalents *by means of example* is thought to be much more helpful than the use of formal analysis. Nevertheless, because it is sometimes desirable to talk, however simply, about the feature after its introduction a number of terms are used and brief generalisations made. It will be noticed that the traditional names for the cases of the noun have been replaced by letter symbols. Other commonly used terms have not been changed. The teacher should normally deal with the substance of the note on the blackboard, using examples selected by the pupils, before they read the note in the text. For an example of the way to do this, see the Commentary on Stage 2.

Reading passages

Principles of reading

(1) Reading denotes primarily the understanding of a portion of written language, ranging from phrases up to the larger units of clause, sentence, paragraph and whole passage. Teaching

methods should, accordingly, help pupils to comprehend at all these levels. It is hoped that the stories themselves will encourage pupils to pursue the meaning from sentence to sentence and that teachers will reinforce, in a variety of ways, the idea that the language makes sense at the large-unit level. Sometimes, when the story situation is strongly dramatic as in Stage 12, a class which is in a hurry to reach the dénouement should be given its head and allowed to read very rapidly just to get the gist of it, before careful re-reading begins. But normally pupils should tackle one or two paragraphs at a time.

(2) We should distinguish between the act of understanding Latin and the various means of testing that understanding, such as comprehension questions and translation into English. It follows that provision has to be made in any reading method for pupils to arrive at some level of understanding *before* the teacher tests for accuracy or completeness. This provision will include:

(*a*) time for pupils to make their own exploration.

(*b*) the minimum necessary clues, particularly vocabulary information.

(3) Reading Latin should include the experience of hearing it read aloud and of reading aloud oneself. If care is taken with pronunciation, valuable benefits accrue. Pleasure is enhanced; appreciation of the rhythms of prose and poetry is developed; and the point is demonstrated that Latin is a foreign language, different from English in sound as well as form. The tape-recording and the marking of long vowels by macrons in the lists of words and phrases will help the pupil, but by far the most potent influence in this matter will be exercised by the teacher.

(4) The act of reading should evoke a personal response to the story, to its characters and its ideas. When the pupil comes to read original authors, his understanding will depend on his ability to perceive abstract ideas and feelings or tones often suggested by a single word or phrase. The maturing of critical sensitivity is a long process, lasting into adult life, and few of our pupils will ever attain a high level of critical power. Nevertheless, this is the direction in which we should help

them to develop (some will surprise us considerably during the last two years of the course, given proper stimulus); and the preparation should begin by our teaching them to react to the concrete situations and boldly delineated personalities in the early stages. The passages themselves, if sufficiently vigorous, will engage the pupils' attention, but the teacher too has a definite role to play. By his questions and incidental comments, arising from his own response to the story, he will lead the pupils beyond the superficial sense of the words. Comments made by pupils, during the school trials, about the character of Caecilius, Grumio, Clemens and others in Unit I showed real capacity to become involved. The fact that their view of these characters also tended to be expressed in fairly crude stereotypes and with some projection of their own attitudes towards adults, simply underlines the teacher's opportunity to begin, cautiously, to guide them toward a more mature judgment.

(5) Pupils should also be guided, when reading the stories, to perceive the evidence about the social and cultural framework of Roman life. The cultural validity aimed at in the stories is not only valuable for its own sake but is also intended to afford a basis for the development of historical thinking. Experience has shown that pupils respond readily to the historical content. They frequently ask questions and make comparisons between Roman and modern life. The paralinguistic sections of the stages are designed to stimulate this reaction and to be used closely with the Latin text. Additional data, to help with answering pupils' questions, are provided in the Stage Commentaries below and more still are available in the works of reference listed in the Bibliography on pages 130–1.

(6) Finally, reading involves a synthesis of all the components outlined above. Pupils need to experience the passage as a whole; and there are various ways of doing this. They include acting, re-reading in groups, listening to a reading by the teacher or to a tape-recording, making a tape-recording or doing a piece of written or art work based on the passage. The main principle of all these possible activities is that they are undertaken after the first reading and form a culmination to it. They

also involve activity on the part of the pupil. Even listening to a dramatic reading by the teacher of a story that has been thoroughly grasped can be an active experience.

Methods of reading

By methods we mean those operations which, when arranged in a suitable sequence, guide pupils to all the levels of reading referred to above and which test the competence of that reading. Two preliminary points should be noted. While there is no one correct sequence of operations, the aim of any sequence that is adopted should be to carry the pupil forward from first explorations to the enjoyment of full understanding. Secondly, the operations concerned with testing should not dominate the method, as often happens in the traditional reading lesson. We now describe a typical sequence with some of the variations that have proved useful.

(1) *Initial presentation*

If an introduction to the story is thought to be necessary, it should merely indicate the setting and not anticipate the events of the story itself. The teacher will then read aloud a portion of the story in Latin to the class. The length of the portion will depend upon the complexity of the story and the ability of the class.

The pace of the initial reading calls for delicate control. For if it is too slow and deliberate, the lesson flags; if it is too hurried, pupils will be hindered in making their first efforts to grasp the meaning. Try to convey something of the meaning by careful emphasis and attention to sense groups. Pupils have their pamphlets open and thus receive the initial presentation simultaneously through ear and eye. An alternative medium is to use the tape-recording at this point.

Some teachers have found that even if the initial presentation is made with the pamphlets closed, many pupils achieve a surprisingly clear understanding and that they enjoy this rather more demanding experience as a variation. We suggest that this variation be used only occasionally and with easy passages. The best time to take in a story by ear alone is at the end of the sequence, not at the beginning.

(2) *Initial exploration*

Next, pupils must be given time to study the passage by themselves and to look for lexical assistance where needed in the list of words and phrases at the end, or if necessary in the vocabulary pamphlet. Teachers sometimes arrange pupils in pairs or groups at this point, so that they can help each other, and we strongly endorse this practice. It cannot be said too often that adequate opportunity for co-operation and social interaction should be given in the classroom and that this should be a normal feature of the methods used.

Until the first exploration has been made by the pupils themselves, the teacher cannot ascertain whether much or little guidance is required of him. When sufficient time has been allowed for exploration, it will often become apparent that many pupils have reached a largely complete understanding by their own efforts.

(3) *Question and answer*

The next step often requires the use of the technique of question and answer. The purpose of this is to check the clarity of the understanding so far achieved and to close remaining gaps. The questioning is directed toward meaning and not to linguistic analysis. For example, a possible sequence of questions that might be asked by the teacher when reading the first paragraph of 'Felix' (Stage 6) is as follows:

> Look at the first sentence. What were the Pompeians doing?
> What were they drinking? Where?
> Were there many or few Pompeians in the inn?
> Look at the second sentence. What did Clemens do?
> Look at the next two sentences. Whom did Clemens see and how did he greet him?
> 'Felix erat libertus.' What does 'libertus' mean and what does it tell us about Felix?

If the replies show marked uncertainty, take the class through each sentence slowly and try to identify the cause of the difficulty. In particular try to distinguish between difficulties that arise from forgetting the meaning of words, and those which are caused by new sentence patterns or such features as suppression, apposition or the predicative use of an adjective. It is at this point that the teacher's detailed knowledge of what is linguistically new or recent is crucial. In dealing with difficulties, there are two main devices which should be employed; first take the pupil back to a familiar sentence that possesses the same structure (the model sentences are usually remembered well) and then ask questions which almost put the answer into pupils' mouths, e.g. 'multi Pompeiani in taberna vinum bibebant'—'there were a lot of people in the inn—who were they? What does "vinum" mean? So what were the Pompeians doing with the wine?' The occasions when so much help has to be given may be relatively few and confined generally to weaker pupils, but the teacher should be ready to use the questioning technique in this way when need arises. It is much more helpful than the 'find the subject, find the verb' approach.

The questioning process has other uses as well. It may be used to guide the class to search for idiomatic English renderings and to lead them away from clumsy or over-literal expressions. It also has the role of stimulating discussion of the human and cultural facets in the story. These two strands, the one arising from universals and the other from historical particularity, are often closely interrelated and in following one, the teacher finds himself handling the other. The readiness of pupils to discuss gladiators or to ask questions about the baths or the theatre often needs a little restraint rather than stimulus. Resist the temptation to spend ten minutes on the Latin and thirty minutes on paralinguistic discussion unless you have planned to do so.

(4) *Translation*

The question of what constitutes an acceptable translation or version is complex. No short answer can be given, but the purpose of the activity is to find out whether the pupil has grasped the sense of a passage clearly or uncertainly. As a method of testing it is an alternative to comprehension questions and one which requires the pupil to show connected and continuous understanding over a series of sentences. It probably plays some part also in reinforcing understanding by confirming to the pupil the correctness of his insight. In assessing a pupil's version, written or oral, the teacher's first concern is to see whether the version shows that the main point has been grasped, reflects clearly enough the facts, situation or argument contained in the Latin and is expressed in a natural English equivalent. Translation is not an exercise whose aim is to reproduce as exactly as possible the form and structure of the original. Sometimes it is possible to combine proximity to the original pattern with acceptable English, but the pupil cannot progress far with reading skill before making the crucial discovery that translation is not a one-for-one process and that it involves judgment and modification. For example:

(a) 'iratissimus erat' may be expressed equally well by
　　　'he was very angry'
　　　'he was furious'
　　　'he was extremely angry'

(b) 'dies erat festus' is not adequately rendered by the literal 'the day was festive'. The obvious idiomatic equivalent is 'it was a holiday'.

Another difficulty with translation is to decide the best moment to do it. As a unit of translation the single sentence is often too short; and it is normally better to postpone it until several sentences or a whole paragraph have been explored and discussed. The pupil may also get more satisfaction from finding his way through a complete paragraph than an isolated sentence. With some stories which are well within the capability of the class and where questioning has shown a high level of understanding, translation may be postponed to the end or omitted altogether.

Some teachers of modern languages are opposed in principle to the practice of translating into English, on the grounds that it encourages the habit of 'inner translation' and prevents the pupil from expressing himself fluently in the new language. The question for Latin teachers is whether this practice inhibits the growth of fluent reading. The view adopted here is that provided it is not over-used and is employed as a check *after* the effort to comprehend has been made, the balance of advantage is in favour of retaining it as a teaching method. It should always be less used than the questioning technique and be balanced by much reading aloud in Latin.

(5) *Consolidation*

After the first reading some further activity is essential to consolidate grasp of the language and perception of its content. This is the point when variations of technique may frequently be practised. Dramatic re-reading by groups of pupils, each taking a different part, has proved to be one of the most stimulating ways of handling a story for a second or third time. The part of the narrator may be read by another group or the rest of the class. Other methods that have been tried successfully include listening to a tape-recording with the pamphlets closed, listening to a dramatic reading by the teacher, pupils making their own recording, and making a written version. This last activity is particularly good for homework, and, because it affords a precise check on individual progress, should be done at fairly regular intervals, namely at least once in every two stages.

Some important variations of reading method

Drama

We have been impressed by the quantity of drama that has been attempted in the classroom during the pre-publication trials, and by the variety of methods used for it.

Some teachers have found that with younger or less able pupils it is desirable to mime the story before acting it in Latin. Miming may take several forms. A group of pupils may mime the action in response to the tape-recording of the Latin; alternatively the teacher or another group of pupils may speak the words to which the action has to be suited. An advantage of this method is that it helps pupils to appreciate the difference between understanding and translation, enabling them to concentrate on the former without the complications of the latter. As a change of activity younger pupils often greatly enjoy making a non-verbal response to linguistic cues.

When the drama is verbal—and this is the usual form—pupils either read their parts from the text or memorise them. Scenery and stage props present no difficulty; they are readily created by imagination after a few preliminary words from the teacher about the setting. An added spice can be given to dramatic readings by recording them on tape and playing them back to the class afterwards. The value of drama for sharpening perception of the interplay between character and event, as well as for reinforcing grasp of language, is such that teachers are recommended to take full advantage of the dramatic potential in the story passages.

Group work

The sequence of operations outlined on pages 16–20 presupposed a lesson which was conducted directly and continuously by the teacher for the greater part of the time. Group work may be introduced as a valuable variation at many points of the sequence. In this, the teacher takes a less direct though still important role.

Experience of the use of group work has, of course, varied. It is by no means an automatic panacea for all the difficulties of the reading lesson. It occasionally happens that one able pupil tends to dominate the group proceedings and so reduce the participation of more passive or less able pupils. But more often, after specific instruction by the teacher in the routines of taking turns, checking and assisting each other, the groups have shown marked ability to function efficiently. The routines are picked up quickly and pupils take pleasure in carrying them out. It is most important in group work to give instructions that are precise and specific; better to say 'Read the story through in Latin, taking turns to read a paragraph and then go through it again with each of you translating a sentence in turn', than the vague directive 'Read through the story and find out what it means'. Some groups have a regular secretary who records the group translation, notes the sentences that have caused difficulty and sees to it that everyone takes his share of the work. The element of social education involved in this method enhances its value, particularly for pupils of retiring personality. Teachers have reported that when groups are in operation, they are able to observe the performance of a substantial number of pupils in any one lesson and to give help to slower learners.

The quantity of Latin read in a group-reading lesson is often surprisingly large; and the involvement of pupils is certainly no less and often rather more than in the teacher-controlled lesson. It is not recommended that groups be composed on the basis of ability but that as far as possible they should be self-selected by the pupils.

In some classrooms the weight and design of the desks restricts the possibility of using this method. Even in such circumstances, however, it is nearly always possible to let pupils read in pairs, taking turns in reading aloud and translating. Some teachers, in fact, prefer pairing to the larger group of four or five.

The manipulation exercises

The exercises that follow the main reading passages provide a change of activity and controlled reinforcement. They give the teacher another check on progress and a means of identifying areas of difficulty.

The main principle of these exercises is that they usually do not aim at testing the advances which have just been introduced, but refer to features that were first encountered two, three or even four stages before. In this way the pupil is kept regularly in contact with important aspects of his recent experiences and given further opportunity to consolidate them. It is, therefore, essential that the teacher be fully aware of the particular point that is being rehearsed in each exercise. Information about this is given in the Stage Commentaries.

The chief type of exercise used is the completion of sentences; in this the pupil has to supply a missing item by selecting it from a given pool of words or phrases. The pupil is also frequently asked to turn the completed sentence or short paragraph into English.

Other types of manipulation include short passages to be tested by either translation or comprehension questions. The standard of difficulty of these passages is kept a little below that of the main passages.

The proportion of time to be allocated to manipulation, including additional exercises that the teacher may devise on the same lines, should not normally exceed 25 per cent of class time and may often be less than this. One homework per week should be given to them. It is intended that they should be worked partly orally and partly in writing. When taking them orally, always ask pupils to respond with a complete sentence; and this should be translated or a question be asked about its meaning.

A note about marking

Written work not only gives a general impression of the progress of individuals but can also be evaluated quantitatively in the form of marks. Two caveats, however, need to be observed. First, some of the manipulation exercises invite a choice not so much between right and wrong, but between the more and the less suitable. These should be marked in such a way as to give credit for a choice which, though not the best, is nevertheless possible and reasonable. In marking translations, especially, there is need to be flexible in assessing the adequacy of the phrase, idiom and structure employed by the pupil. A rendering which closely parallels the Latin structure may be easier to mark but may also be less adequate in conveying clearly the sense of the original. Similarly, errors of a merely lexical nature should not be penalised as heavily as misunderstanding of the essential structure —for example, confusion of subject and object.

The second caveat concerns the use and interpretation of marks. Marks may be used—and properly—to measure the accuracy and success of a piece of work against a fixed standard or norm. Quantitative assessment of this kind may show that all the pupils in the class are doing well or badly, or that a few are being very successful while the majority are at a lower level. Such data are useful. But the marks may also be used to compare pupils with each other and to produce orders of relative merit. These are less useful in ordinary teaching situations, because they are frequently misunderstood. The child who is placed first in the class may be given an exaggerated view of his success; the child who is placed bottom may take this to indicate failure when, in fact, his performance may be at least satisfactory. The teacher may also make the error of supposing that the intervals separating each point in the order of merit have the same value, and thus overlook the possibility that the distribution of attainment is heavily bunched in the middle. The difference between the tenth and twentieth position may be minimal, while the gap between the first and fourth position may be wide in terms of actual performance.

For this reason it is recommended that the use of marks for inter-pupil comparisons or for stimulating pupil competition should be allowed much less prominence than has often been accorded to it. More emphasis ought to be laid upon comparing the individual against his own past performance and with fixed norms.

Finally, we make the simple point that a pupil's mistakes are as important as his successes in revealing his grasp of the subject. To dismiss errors as 'careless', or to attribute them merely to stupidity, may be to overlook a significant clue about the concepts which are difficult or incomprehensible to the pupil. Dispassionate analysis by the teacher of common errors made by one or a group of pupils is essential if real progress is to be made.

23

The paralinguistic material

One of the major aims of the Course is to widen pupils' knowledge of classical civilisation. It is for this reason that stories are set in an ancient context and their content is explained and amplified at the end of each stage.

What is meant by 'widening the pupils' knowledge of classical civilisation'? At the lowest level this may be interpreted as the passive reception and memorisation of facts given. But few, if any, teachers would consider this interpretation appropriate in itself to their pupils' intelligence or indeed to the subject.

We suggest that the following objectives, already being pursued in many schools, should be kept in mind. Pupils should be encouraged to:

(a) make comparisons between the ancient and modern worlds,
(b) ask for and suggest explanations of the facts presented in the pamphlets,
(c) produce original work of their own; this may take the form of an imaginative essay or of drawing conclusions from the facts they have acquired,
(d) realise what is involved in making valid judgments, whether they be historical, aesthetic or moral.

It is not suggested that children of eleven and twelve will be able to proceed very far with (d), but it is better to err on the side of over-ambition than to underestimate the capacity and interests of young adolescents.

Some teachers are pursuing these objectives in class discussions and by setting written work that extends the intellect and imagination. Others have been agreeably surprised by their pupils' talent for model-making, art and dramatic work. Most of these activities are best done in pairs or groups. In order to assist this active handling of the material we have included suggestions for activities in the Stage Commentaries. Not all teachers will be able to put them into practice, but even where time is very short, it is hoped that one or two important topics will be chosen for special consideration with the class.

The position of the paralinguistic section at the end of each pamphlet does not mean that it should always be taken last. In some stages, it will clearly be desirable for pupils to have read it before work begins on the stories, in order to clarify ideas expressed in the Latin. The initial reading will perhaps normally be done by pupils on their own, probably as homework. The ensuing discussion need not occupy a whole lesson; it may be associated with a particular story or combined with the showing of appropriate slides.

4 Pronunciation

No attempt has been made in this section to describe the actual quality of consonants and vowels. Teachers are referred for guidance to the tape and to W. S. Allen's *Vox Latina* (Cambridge University Press, 1965).

Length of vowels

It is essential in Latin to distinguish between long and short vowels. (There are also differences of quality, and differences from English speech habits, but the distinction of length of vowel is fundamental.) There are some rules of general application, e.g.

(1) final vowels (i.e. when the word ends with a vowel, not a consonant) are usually consistent in quantity in accordance with the significance of the inflexion, e.g. -ĕ in 3rd decl. abl. sing. and present infinitive active, but -ē in 5th decl. abl. sing. and most adverbs formed from 1st/2nd decl. adj.

For a full list, refer to a grammar, e.g. Kennedy's *Revised Latin Primer* (Longmans, new edn, 1962), p. 202.

(2) other vowels

    (*a*) a vowel immediately preceding another vowel in the same word is usually short, unless the two vowels form a diphthong (*ae, au, oe* are normally diphthongs). Thus ĕadem, but āēdem; tŭa, but taūrum; mĕos, but mōēnia. Both *eu* and *ui*, which are usually disyllabic, sometimes occur as diphthongs, e.g. seū, but aurĕus; huīc, but terrŭit.

    (*b*) apart from characteristic stem vowels, e.g. amāre, amābat, amāvit, and apart from words derived from the same root which often preserve the same quantity (e.g. nāvis, nāvigare), *nearly all other vowels must be learned individually for the word concerned*, either from the tape or from the words and phrases lists, marked for this purpose, in the pupil's pamphlets.

Quantity of syllables

The quantity of syllables (as distinct from the length of vowels) may be summarised as follows:

a *heavy* syllable is one containing a long vowel or a diphthong, e.g. le-*gē*-tis, pu-el-l*ǣ*;

or containing a short vowel immediately followed by two consonants, e.g. le-*gĕn*-tis, pu-*ĕl*-lae.

a *light* syllable is one containing a short vowel, followed by another vowel or a single consonant, e.g. *pŭ*-el-lae, le-*gĭ*-tis.

Note (1) For these purposes, the consonants need not be in the same word as the vowel.

(2) *h* does not count as a consonant; *x* and *z* each count as two consonants.

(3) An exception, in spoken Latin, was the combination of a plosive (*p, t, c, b, d* or *g*) and liquid (*r* or *l*) following a short final vowel or a short vowel in the same word; this combination gave normally a light syllable, e.g. thus usually te-*nĕ*-brae (light), rarely te-*nĕb*-rae (heavy).

Accent

Most scholars nowadays agree in believing that the Latin word-accent was primarily a stress accent, falling according to the following rules:

(*a*) disyllables carry an accent on their first syllable, e.g. hóstis;

(*b*) polysyllables carry an accent on the penultimate syllable, if this is of heavy quantity, and on the antepenultimate (regardless of quantity), if the penultimate is light, e.g. salúte, sapiéntis, but mílite, socíetas.

Verse rhythms as well as word-accent depend on the quantity of syllables. It is important therefore to understand the distinction between length of vowels and quantity of syllables. Observation of correct vowel-length and careful articulation of consonants (particularly double consonants, each of which is pronounced separately) will ensure the correct quantities of syllables and assist the placing of the accent.

E.g. in amícus, the *i* is long, the containing syllable is heavy and therefore carries the word-accent.

In ingéntes, although the first *e* is short, the containing syllable is heavy (two consonants following), and therefore carries the word-accent.

In áccidit (=it happens), although the *a* is short, the first syllable is heavy because the *c* is pronounced double. The penultimate syllable contains a short *i*, and therefore the accent falls on the first syllable. Contrast this with accídit (=he cuts) and accíngit.

Marking of pupil's text

In the stage pamphlets, long vowels (but not diphthongs) are marked with a macron in the lists of words and phrases.

5 Slides of Pompeii and Herculaneum

The teacher's kit contains sixty colour slides of Pompeii and Herculaneum. Each slide is listed below with a note about its location, subject and other points of interest. They are arranged in groups according to theme. Further information about the slides, which may be useful for classroom discussion, will be found in the books mentioned in the Bibliography.

Private houses

Main living areas

1 Naples Museum. Bronze portrait bust of Lucius Caecilius Iucundus. A copy of this 'herm' stands in the atrium of his house, just outside the entrance to the tablinum.
2 Pompeii. Vestibule of house. This 'cave canem' mosaic is on the floor of the vestibule of the House of the Tragic Poet. The two entrances on either side of the vestibule led to rooms which were used as shops. Other more friendly expressions of welcome, such as AVE, are not uncommon in the vestibule of Pompeian houses.
3 Pompeii. House of Menander. The atrium. This, and the next slide, give an impression of the atrium of a substantial town house. This view is taken from the tablinum looking toward the ianua. Notice particularly (a) the compluvium, the opening in the roof, a feature which dates back to the earliest form of Italian house. Its original functions were to admit light and allow smoke from the domestic fire to escape; (b) the impluvium, let into the floor, which caught rain-water entering through the compluvium.
4 Pompeii. House of Menander. The atrium. The view is taken from one corner of the atrium looking across to the lararium in the opposite corner. The vestibulum is just visible on the right. Notice the remains of red decorative panels on the walls and the

29

darkness of the cubicula opening off the atrium. The circular stone lid, flush with the floor on the far side of the impluvium, covers the underground cistern in which water flowing from the impluvium was stored for domestic use.

5 Pompeii. House of Menander. Lararium. All houses, rich and poor, had a shrine dedicated to the lares which guarded the domestic hearth. Offerings of food were placed there each day.

6 Pompeii. House of Caecilius. Lararium. The marble relief pictures the earthquake of A.D. 62, and refers to the forum. On the left the Arch of Drusus and the Temple of Jupiter, flanked by equestrian statues, are shown toppling sideways; to the right is an altar and sacrificial scene.

7 Herculaneum. House with screen. The atrium. This house is so called because of its fine wooden screen separating the atrium from the tablinum. The timber has survived in carbonised form. In the eruption of A.D. 79 Herculaneum was not bombarded like Pompeii with lapilli and ash, but was submerged in a tide of volcanic mud. This helped to preserve much of the timber work and upper stories of houses in Herculaneum.

8 Herculaneum. House with screen. The impluvium with fountain in the middle. The two levels, representing an older and a newer impluvium, can be seen clearly.

9 Pompeii. House of Trebius. Summer triclinium. This is one of many open-sided dining-rooms found in the peristyles of Pompeian houses. Notice the fixed concrete couches on which cushions would be placed, and the small round table in the middle.

10 Herculaneum. Sundial. Sundials were imported by the Romans from the Greek world. They were later supplemented by water clocks. The dial is calibrated into twelve units, marking the hours from sunrise to sunset.

11 Pompeii. House of Loreius. Loggia. The summer triclinium was at the far end of this loggia; and a magnificent series of water channels and fountains made his garden one of the most beautiful in Pompeii. Notice the vine-covered wooden framework that replaced the usual peristyle here.

12 Pompeii. House of Loreius. Marble hound and deer. A detail from slide 11.

13 Pompeii. House of the Vettii. Garden and fountains. This garden of one of the most famous houses in Pompeii has been restored as far as possible to its original condition.

14 Pompeii. House of the Vettii. Fountain. Detail from slide 13. A system of lead pipes supplied the fountains with water.

Decoration

15 Pompeii. Decorative wall panel. Architectural motifs were frequently used and gave an impression of open vistas and spaciousness.

16 Naples Museum. Wall painting. Hare with grapes. The Pompeians often decorated the walls of their dining-rooms with pictures of fruit and game.

17 Naples Museum. Wall painting. Fruit in glass bowl.

18 Naples Museum. Wall painting. Peacock on trellis. Peacocks were not only kept to grace gardens, but also appeared as a delicacy on the menu.

19 Pompeii. Wall painting. Roman warships. In the atrium of the House of the Vettii.

20 Herculaneum. Mosaic of Neptune and Amphitrite. This mosaic is on the wall of a nymphaeum in the house of a prosperous wine merchant.

Furniture and domestic utensils

21 Herculaneum. House with screen. Bed in cubiculum. The bed would have had a mattress, blankets and a pillow. Bedrooms were usually small and sparsely furnished.

22 Naples Museum. Arca. This was the type of container in which family records and valuables would be stored. It stood in the tablinum or atrium. Compare with the chests to be seen in many parish churches in England.

23 Pompeii. House of the Vettii. Kitchen stove. The fuel was normally wood or charcoal. This was burned in the top of the stove; the pots stood on metal grids directly above the burning fuel. The space beneath the stove was used for storing the fuel. Domestic cooking usually took the form of boiling, grilling or frying. Separate baking ovens are also found, but not so frequently. Most Pompeians obtained baked food from a nearby bakery.

24 Pompeii. Wall painting. Silver dining service. This picture of an elaborate dining service is on the wall of a tomb situated just outside the Vesuvius gate.

25 Naples Museum. Lamp standard. Artificial light was obtained by lighting a wick projecting from a container of oil. These lamps were made of pottery or metal. A considerable number must have been needed to illuminate large rooms, and banquets must frequently have been eaten in a very smoky atmosphere.

26 Naples Museum. Lamps. Wicks were inserted in the holes nearest the camera.

Streets and shops

27 Pompeii. The sea-gate. The small thoroughfare for pedestrians, the large for animals and vehicles. It was closed at sunset.

28 Pompeii. Strada dell'Abbondanza. View of the main east–west street, looking east from the point at which it left the forum. The wall on the left foreground belongs to the Eumachia, the guild-hall of the fullers. In the middleground, on the left side of the road, is one of the numerous street fountains. In the distance the road curves a little before reaching the central cross-roads.

29 Pompeii. Road junction and stepping stones. This is the central junction where the north–south street (via di Stabia) crosses the east–west street (strada dell'Abbondanza). The stepping stones enabled pedestrians to avoid the garbage that collected in the roadway. The gaps between the stones allowed the passage of carts.

30 Pompeii. Narrow street. This is the vicolo del Lupanare, a narrow street running north from the strada dell'Abbondanza at a point just east of the forum.

31 Pompeii. Street junction and house with balcony. The street on the left is the same as that photographed from the other end in slide 29. A number of houses in Pompeii and Herculaneum have a balcony projecting over the street. An interesting example of the use of a wide-angle camera lens.

32 Pompeii. Tethering hole in kerbstone. These holes, pierced at intervals through the pavement kerbs, were used for tethering animals.

33 Pompeii. Shop shutter and strada dell'Abbondanza. This is a concrete cast of the original timber shutter. It was drawn sideways along a groove in the stone threshold. Notice the small door let into the right-hand end of the shutter. This shopkeeper locked up before he fled from the eruption.

34 Pompeii. Shop sign. Dairy. A carved plaque was the usual way of indicating the business conducted in the shop. The goat was the normal sign for a dairy.

35 Pompeii. Thermopolium. Hot drinks of mulled wine could be bought here. Jars containing the drinks stood in the deep containers let into the counter. Bars like these would also serve snacks and light meals.

36 Pompeii. Wine press. This reconstructed press is located in the Villa of the Mysteries, half a mile north of Pompeii. The lever, which was pulled downwards by ropes, exerted pressure on the squeezing boards on the top of the vat. The juice of the grapes ran out of the bottom of the vat along a channel by the wall and then down into large amphorae. These were stored in underground vaults.

37 Pompeii. House of the Vettii. Cupids making and selling perfume. This is a section of the 'amorini' panel on the wall of the large dining-room of this house. The cupids offer perfume to the seated woman who sniffs it on her wrist. Her slave girl stands behind her.

The forum and business activity

38 Pompeii. Forum, from S.E. The temple of Jupiter at the far end, Vesuvius beyond. This large open space, measuring approximately 124 feet by 446 feet, and surrounded by the major public buildings, was the religious, political and economic centre of the city.

39 Pompeii. Forum from N.W. This view gives some impression of its size. In the background are the remains of the curia.

40 Pompeii. Forum. North entrance. On the left, the wall of the temple of Jupiter. Notice the 'cippi' or barrier stones under the arch, stopping the entry of wheeled traffic.

41 Pompeii. Forum. West colonnade, from the curia.

42 Pompeii. Forum. Table of weights. This 'mensa ponderaria' stood in a recess on the west side of the forum. Originally it contained twelve cavities giving the standards for liquid and dry measures. In the pre-Roman period the measures were Greek, but were enlarged about 20 B.C. to conform to the Roman standard. Compare with the weights and measures departments of our local authorities.

43 Naples Museum. Painting of coins and tablets. The Pompeians seem to have painted every aspect and detail of their lives. Compare this with the range of content in our popular art.

44 Pompeii. Wall painting. Merchant ship. Compare the squat, bulging lines of this merchantman with the sleekness of the trireme.

45 Pompeii. House of the Vettii. Cupids making coins. On the right, cupids melting down metal in the furnace; on the left, a craftsman at work.

46 Pompeii. The large theatre. Auditorium and orchestra. View from the stage. Seating for 5,000. Awnings could be spread over a large part of the auditorium by ropes and pulleys to protect spectators from the sun. The wide seats of the lowest tier were reserved for magistrates, decurions and local nobility.

47 Naples Museum. Painting of tragic actor. An actor prepares for a performance, while a slave holds his mask.

48 Pompeii. Relief of comic mask. Relief found in the house of the 'Golden Cupids'. This house had a private acting stage on one side of the peristyle; the owner presumably staged private performances of plays for his friends.

49 Naples Museum. Mosaic of a chorus interlude in New Comedy. Two men, one with cymbals, another with a tambourine, are dancing to the music of a woman flute-player, who is accompanied by a dwarf. They are all wearing actors' masks and tights. The mosaic is thought to be a copy of a Greek painting, now lost.

50 Pompeii. The amphitheatre. Exterior staircase. The interior was not photographed owing to its extremely dilapidated and overgrown condition.

51 Pompeii. Wall painting of gladiators.

52 Naples Museum. Gladiator's helmet, decorated with dolphins.

53   Naples Museum. Gladiator's shoulder pad. This piece of armour
     was worn by a retiarius.
54   Naples Museum. Gladiator's greaves.

The baths

55   Pompeii. Stabian baths. The apodyterium. A good example of
     the undressing room of the public baths. Clothes were placed in
     the niches and guarded by public slaves. The next three slides
     are all of the women's baths at Herculaneum, since these have
     survived in rather better condition than others.
56   Herculaneum. Baths. Detail of a mosaic. This picture of a squid
     is part of the mosaic on the floor of the apodyterium.
57   Herculaneum. Baths. The caldarium. The water in the bath was
     kept hot by a furnace below. The whole room would be very
     warm and steamy. A basin of cold water stood at the end
     opposite the bath, where the bathers could get a cold rinse-
     down before leaving. Notice the barrel vaulting. The curved ribs
     moulded on the ceiling would help to conduct the water, result-
     ing from the condensation of steam, away to the side of the room.
58   Herculaneum. Baths. Marble bench in the caldarium. Through the
     doorway can be seen the tepidarium with a fine geometric mosaic.
59   Naples Museum. Strigils and oil pots. Bathers brought their own
     equipment and towels to the baths. Olive oil was the equivalent
     of soap: it was rubbed into the skin, where it combined with dirt
     and impurities. It was then scraped off gently with the strigil.
     Notice how the shape of the strigil conforms well to its function.

Vesuvius

60   Volcanic steam in the crater of Vesuvius, dormant, but not
     dead. The ancients associated volcanoes, especially Mount
     Etna in Sicily, with Vulcan, the god of fire, who forged
     the thunderbolts of Jupiter deep in the bowels of the earth.
     Vesuvius had been dormant for centuries before A.D. 79. Its
     sides were wooded and used for vine growing and grazing. Since
     79, it has erupted violently on several occasions, the last time
     being in 1944.

The use of slides

Ideally the slides should be shown as and when the content of a stage requires them. In practice, however, such flexible use is often not possible, and the teacher has to plan a session with slides well in advance. Even so, it is wise to limit the number shown at a sitting and to select them in a way that enables one to explore a topic. If too many are shown at a time or insufficient interpretation is given by the teacher, much of their value will be lost and viewing then can become tedious to the pupils. Time should be allowed for pupils' questions. The discussion should be related, where appropriate, to the content of the Latin stories and the paralinguistic section of the pupil's pamphlet. One teacher, during the classroom trials, developed an interesting additional use of the slides: as a test of pupils' paralinguistic knowledge he projected a slide for a few moments, then asked the class to write down answers to his questions about it. This was repeated with a number of slides. Needless to say, the test was a popular one.

For reasons of economy, the slides have not been mounted between glass. Reasonable care should be taken to avoid overheating a slide by leaving it too long in the projector. When putting slides into the projector, stand behind the projector facing toward the screen, place the slide into the carrying frame with the black dot in the top right-hand corner position. Some projectors, such as the Rank Aldis 1000, are designed for use in daylight conditions, but direct sunlight entering the room will inevitably reduce the colour of the image even when a projector of this kind is being used. Subdued lighting is always preferable. Other projectors with a lamp of lower power will need more reduction of daylight. Complete blackout, however, is a convenience rather than a necessity.

Remember to test the projector before using it, and to allow it to cool down after use before moving it. When hot, the lamp is particularly liable to damage if the projector is knocked or shaken.

6 The Tape-recording

The tape has been recorded at 3¾ i.p.s., and may be played on any tape-recorder capable of accepting a 5-inch reel. The tape is two-track, which means that it has been recorded on both sides of the tape.

The following material from Unit I has been recorded:

Stage 1   Model sentences
Stage 2   Model sentences
          'coquus in triclinio cenat'
Stage 3   'venalicius'
Stage 4   'Hermogenes'
Stage 5   Model sentences
          'Poppaea amicum exspectat'
Stage 6   Model sentences
          'Felix et fur'
Stage 7   Model sentences
          'fabula mirabilis'
          'post cenam'
Stage 8   Model sentences
          'in arena'
          'venatio'
Stage 9   Model sentences
          'in palaestra'
          'ad thermas'
Stage 10 Model sentences
          'controversia'
Stage 11 Model sentences
          'Lucius Spurius Pomponianus'
Stage 12 Model sentences
          All the story passages

The method of recording

(1) Each item on the tape is introduced by the number of the stage and a title. For example, 'Stage 1—Model sentences'; 'Stage 6—Felix et fur'; 'Stage 9—in palaestra'.

(2) In Stages 1 and 2 each model sentence is repeated twice on the tape. There is a short pause between the utterances. After Stage 2 the model sentences are given only once.

(3) Throughout the tape the narrative passages are recorded with only one utterance of each sentence.

Handling the tape

When using the tape in a way that requires pupils to repeat each utterance aloud after hearing it (this exercise will normally be done only with the model sentences), it is necessary to have a pause long enough to allow the class to make the response. The teacher must create these pauses by operating the pause or stop control on the recorder. This will provide a more flexible means of control than would have been possible if a pause of fixed length had been built into the tape. The short pauses on the tape allow the teacher time to operate the pause or stop control.

Purpose of the tape

The tape is an aid only, and will not be the major vehicle for the communication of the sound of Latin in the classroom. The voices of the teacher and pupils will be heard more often than the tape, but it should play a helpful and stimulating role. This role is threefold:

(1) to consolidate the awareness and enjoyment of a passage as a whole, after initial comprehension has been established. The recording of the narrative passages will help to set a standard of vigour and liveliness for the pupils' own reading aloud.

(2) to reinforce perception of sense groups and of the sentence as the primary unit of meaning.

(3) to guide both teacher and pupils in the reproduction of the correct sounds of words. Although our knowledge of those sounds is inevitably incomplete, much more is known about

them today than formerly and it is most desirable that this knowledge should be communicated through classroom practice.

A further consideration is that pupils vary in their preference for visual or aural stimuli to memory. Some associate the sense of a word or phrase with its sound rather more easily than with its purely visual form. These variations in verbal sensitivity should be catered for by assuring that sound is not neglected in the classroom.

Teaching sequences

Model sentences

The tape may be used for the initial presentation of the sentence, but care must be taken not to allow it to obscure the primary task, which is to establish by question and answer what the sentence means. It will probably usually be better to postpone practice with the tape until this task has been achieved. Use the tape normally after a block or all of the sentences have been read at least once. Then, with the pupils' pamphlets open or closed according to your preference, proceed as follows:

Teacher: 'Listen to the sentence on the tape and in the pause that follows repeat it aloud together. After you have said it, I will say it so that you may hear it again.' (Note: in Stages 1 and 2 the tape will provide the second utterance, thereafter the teacher must supply it.)

Tape: First utterance. Teacher operates pause control.

Class: Response. Vary the response group: sometimes the whole class, sometimes part of the class.

Teacher: Second utterance. Class listens and compares their performance. It may sometimes be useful to have a second response from the class at this point.
Proceed to the next sentence.

N.B. This activity should never occupy a whole lesson. Ten minutes in one lesson is recommended as the maximum.

Reading passages

Again, the tape should be used as a supplement at or near the end of a reading lesson. The recording of the stories is intended to stimulate

appreciation, not as an exercise to be performed by pupils in reproducing the sounds. The pace of the recording is quite brisk and pupils
should normally have their text open while they are listening to it.
But you may certainly experiment with having it closed; be guided
by class reaction.

Two main sequences are suggested:

(1) class listens to whole passage without pause or interruption.
They then close texts and teacher leads a discussion by
question and answer about the story (its characters, climax,
mood and points of paralinguistic interest).

or (2) class listens to a portion: perhaps a few sentences, perhaps a
paragraph. Teacher operates pause control and questions class
briefly to check understanding and to fill in background
atmosphere. Then proceed to the next portion.

7 The Linguistic Notation

The linguistic foundation of the Course consists of sentence patterns that develop in a carefully controlled sequence from two basic patterns to the normal complexity of literary Latin. While this treatment receives no formal discussion in the pupil's text, it is desirable for the teacher to know what patterns are introduced and rehearsed in the text. Information about this is given at the beginning of each Stage Commentary; and to express it in a concise way, a new system of notation has been employed. Unfamiliarity may at first give it an appearance of complexity, but with a little practice it soon becomes familiar and assists one to see the language from a structural point of view. The notation is explained below with examples.

One change from traditional description, however, requires special mention. Both here and in the pupil's text the usual case names of the noun have been replaced by letters. Capital letters represent nouns, small letters represent adjectives. This has been done partly to facilitate the expression of nouns and adjectives within the notational system, and partly to reduce the number of technical words with which the pupil is confronted. Many teachers have found that A, B, C, etc. are easier for pupils to grasp than the traditional nomenclature. In Unit I the nominative, accusative, dative and ablative cases are used. The ablative case, however, occurs only in the context of prepositional phrases in this unit. Its other uses are deferred until Unit III. The genitive case is introduced in Unit II. This difference in the order of introducing the cases is reflected in the letter sequence by which they are labelled. (For the principles underlying the linguistic scheme the reader is referred to Appendix A.)

General symbols

S   sentence pattern
Cl   subordinate clause
Q   qualifying phrase; this is subdivided where appropriate into I—invariable qualifier, e.g. adverb, X—prepositional phrase
N   nominal phrase

V   verbal phrase
=   'sum' or other parts of the verb 'to be'

Cases

	nouns		adjectives
	A	nominative	a
	B	accusative	b
	C	dative	c
	D	genitive	d
	E	ablative	e

Note. The vocative is used, but is not handled within the case system.

Persons of the verb

	singular	plural
	1/	/1
	2/	/2
	3/	/3

Singular/plural: these are represented by the position of the oblique stroke /. Thus A/ (vir) as opposed to /A (viri).

Examples of the notation

N.B. On no account should this notation be taught to pupils.

Sentence patterns

There are two basic patterns from which the development proceeds.

    S i (the equational sentence)

e.g.	A = A	Caecilius est argentarius.
	= CA	est mercatoribus candidatus optimus.

    S ii (the operational sentence)

e.g.	V	ridet.
	AV	mercator ridet.
	BV	amicos laudabat.
	ABV	mercator amicos laudavit.
	CV	mihi placet.
	ACV	Marcus Holconio credebat.
	ACBV	Metella Quinto togam emit.

Phrases

The qualifying phrase (Q)

AQV	Cerberus ferociter latrat.
	coquus in horto sedebat.
AQBV	Pompeiani saepe actores laudabant.
ABQV	bestiarii leones in arena necaverunt.
AQQV	coquus in triclinio magnifice cenat.

The nominal phrase

A	Caecilius
A × 2	Caecilius et Metella
aA	magnus leo
B	amicum
B × 2	gladiatorem et amicum
Bb	amicum meum

Morphology

A	A/	amicus, puella, mercator, civis
	/A	amici, puellae, mercatores, cives
B	B/	nuntium, ancillam, pastorem
	/B	nuntios, ancillas, pastores
E	E/	horto, villa, mercatore
	/E	hortis, villis, mercatoribus
V	1/	contendo	/1	contendimus
	2/	contendis	/2	contenditis
	3/	contendit	/3	contendunt

Stage Commentaries

Stage 1

Linguistic information

Input			*Examples*
sentence	S i	A = A	Caecilius est pater.
		A = Q	servus est in horto.
sentence	S ii	AV	Grumio coquit.
		AQV	canis in via dormit.
phrase	Q	X	in horto
morphology	noun	A/	-us (servus), -a (Metella)
			-ens (Clemens), -io (Grumio)
			-is (canis), -er (pater)
	noun	E/	-o (atrio), -a (via)
	verb	3/	-at (intrat), -et (sedet)
			-it (surgit, dormit)

Model sentences

Content

These introduce Caecilius and the members of his household. Many of the stories in Unit I are written round these characters, and it is interesting to notice the varied attitudes which many pupils develop toward them. There is no 'approved interpretation'. Pupils should be entirely free to view the characters in their own way.

Aim

To introduce S i and S ii in their basic forms, and a selection of the most common morphology.

Method

For suggestions about methods of presenting and handling the model sentences see pages 11–13. For the pronunciation of proper names see Appendix B on page 125. These sentences are on the tape-recording. Look out for the following minor difficulties which sometimes occur:

(1) The absence of a definite or indefinite article in Latin may confuse pupils for a time. Help pupils to select the appropriate article for the context.

(2) 'servus in horto laborat' (and similar sentences) is sometimes translated by 'the slave is in the garden working', perhaps by analogy with 'servus est in horto'. Do not reject this rendering, but ask for other ways of expressing it in English and guide pupils toward 'the slave is working' or 'the slave works'. Pupils will soon come to prefer the latter versions.

(3) Some common nouns, e.g. 'coquus', 'amicus', are treated as proper names by some pupils for a while.

Reading passage

Content

A short story about Cerberus the dog and Grumio the cook. Point out the growling sound of the name 'Cerberus' by vigorous rolling of the 'r's. Mention may be made of his mythological ancestor. Compare him also with the 'cave canem' slide (no. 2) which shows the mosaic of the dog in the vestibule of the House of the Tragic Poet in Pompeii.

Method

For a general discussion of reading techniques see pages 13–21. It might be helpful to illustrate this story with blackboard drawings. At suitable points in the story the teacher could draw a quick sketch, using simple outline or pin-figures, and ask the class to identify and read out the relevant sentence or sentences. Members of the class may then be invited to come out and draw a sentence on the board for the others to identify. Alternatively the story could be mimed—on the second reading—by a group of pupils while another group reads out the text. Activities of this kind are particularly helpful as consolidation for younger pupils. The drawings and groundplan of a Pompeian house in this stage should be used to give a visual interpretation of such phrases as 'in atrio', 'in tablino', 'in culina'.

Manipulation exercises

An important feature of the manipulation exercises is that many of them depend primarily on sense discrimination. Pupils should be encouraged to select the option which makes the best sense; and answers which, though structurally feasible, make poor sense, should be discouraged.

Exercise	*Criterion of choice*	*Pattern rehearsed*	
I	sense	S i	A = Q
2	sense	S ii	AQV
3	sense	S i, S ii	A = Q, AQV

Paralinguistic

Content

This section tries to establish Lucius Caecilius Iucundus as a Roman citizen and a successful business man. He occupies a substantial town house and is served by numerous slaves over whom he has nearly absolute rights (ius vitae necisque). The house is situated in a dignified residential quarter, just north of the junction between via di Stabia and strada di Nola (topographical references to Pompeian streets will be given in their usual Italian form, references to house names in the English equivalent). On the archaeological grid map (to be found in A. Maiuri, *Pompeii*, Ist. Geografico de Agostini, 1960, and *Guide to Pompeii*, Libreria dello Stato, 1964; and in M. Brion, *Pompeii and Herculaneum*, Elek Books, 1960), it is Regio v, Insula I, number 26. The house was large and well appointed, but in its present condition is rather unexciting apart from the lararium and the bronze portrait bust (original in Naples Museum) to be found in the atrium. The lararium is decorated with marble panels showing in bas-relief scenes of the disastrous earthquake of A.D. 62 which laid much of the town in ruins. The first panel shows the Temple of Jupiter, the adjacent arch of Drusus and two equestrian statues about to collapse, an altar, and a bull being led to sacrifice (slide 6). The second panel shows the Vesuvius Gate, only a few yards from Caecilius' front door, on the point of falling.

Our knowledge of Caecilius derives also from the important

collection of business records on waxed tablets discovered in a strong box (arca) in his house in 1875 (*C.I.L.* IV, Supp. Part I). The following examples indicate the range and diversity of his interests:

	Sesterces
Loan	1,450
Sale of timber	1,985
Sale of land	35,270
Rent of fullery	1,652
Grazing land rented from the town council	2,675
Auction of linen on behalf of Egyptian merchant	[amount not stated]

The drawing and plan of a Pompeian house given in the pupil's text are a simplification to show the essential components of the 'domus urbana'. In fact Caecilius' house was more complex than this. When pupils have become familiar with the basic lay-out, they should be given an opportunity to study and interpret the plans of actual Pompeian houses. Plans may be found, for example, in E. Paoli, *Rome—its People, Life and Customs* (Longmans, 1963), chapter 2.

Suggested activities

(1) Discuss with the class the different sources of our knowledge about Caecilius. You might also ask pupils, 'If our civilisation were destroyed, how could archaeologists in the future find out about our way of life?'

(2) 'Imagine you are a business friend of Caecilius and are also interested in other people's houses. Write an account of a visit you make to Caecilius at home.' Ask pupils to include people and dialogue in the writing. Before this activity, some relevant slides should be shown and talked about.

(3) Show some plans of actual houses and invite pupils to use their knowledge to interpret the main features. A selection of plans will be found in Brion, Maiuri, and Paoli.

(4) Discuss points of contrast between modern dwellings and the Pompeian 'domus urbana'. Besides the differences of lay-out, discuss reasons for the more inward-looking character of the Pompeian

house; consider also the means of running it—slaves, types of fuel and appliances for heating and lighting.

(5) For younger pupils the idea of a 'time machine' that takes them back to Pompeii in A.D. 79 can be a stimulus to imaginative writing, centred on the paralinguistic material.

Stage 2

Linguistic information

Previous input			Examples
sentence	S i	A = A	Metella est mater.
		A = Q	mater est in atrio.
sentence	S ii	AV	Grumio stertit.
		AQV	coquus in culina dormit.
phrase	Q	X (preposition + noun)	in triclinio
morphology	noun	A/	-us, -is, -er, etc.
		E/	-o, -a
	verb	3/	-at, -et, -it

New input			Examples
sentence	S ii	ABV	amicus Caecilium salutat.
		ABQV	coquus cibum in mensa videt.
		AQQV	coquus in triclinio magnifice cenat.
phrase	Q	I (invariable)	suaviter, magnifice
morphology	noun	A/	-o (pavo), -or (mercator)
		B/	-um (amicum)
			-am (ancillam)
			-em (pavonem)

Note (1) The suppression of an explicit subject (A) is very common in Latin, more so than in English. This feature is introduced gradually into the pupil's material, beginning with very easy examples. In Stage 2 it is limited to the following patterns:

ABV + V, 'Grumio triclinium intrat et circumspectat.'
ABV + BV, 'Grumio cibum consumit et vinum bibit.'

The B item following 'et' is temporarily restricted to inanimate or impersonal nouns. Pupils are not expected to find any difficulty with suppression at this stage, but the teacher is recommended to observe carefully how pupils cope with it and to be ready to assist if necessary.

(2) The negative 'non', the conjunction 'et', the particle 'quoque', exclamations and vocatives are omitted, for the sake of simplicity, from the description of sentence patterns. Similarly, words such as 'sed', 'tamen', 'nam', when they are introduced in the text, are not recorded as structural items.

Model sentences

Content

On pages 3 and 4 a friend visits Caecilius and the scene is set in the atrium. On pages 5 and 6 Metella superintends operations in the kitchen. 'salutat' means to greet, by word or in writing, in the sense of 'wish health to'. 'salve' was used on meeting, occasionally at parting. Besides this general use, 'salutat' also denotes the formal act of calling on somebody to pay one's respects to him; hence 'salutatio' is the morning visit made by clients to their patrons. The pictures show the friend extending his hand in greeting.

Aim

To introduce S ii in the pattern ABV.

Method

Introduce the situation briefly, 'Here we have a friend (amicus) visiting Caecilius.' Then take each pair of sentences together, in the following manner:

(1) Ask class to identify the single character in the left-hand picture and translate the caption. This should present no difficulty, as the sentence patterns were experienced in Stage 1.

(2) Next turn to the right-hand picture, explore the situation with such questions as, 'Who is approaching Caecilius?' 'What is he doing?'

(3) Invite suggestions for the meaning of the caption 'amicus Caecilium salutat'. Various interpretations of 'salutat' will be offered, such as 'greets', 'says hello to', 'salutes'. Any of these renderings will have the effect of establishing the appropriate grammatical relationship between 'amicus' and 'Caecilium'.

No analysis of the form of 'Caecilium' should be attempted at this point.

(4) Repeat the process with the next pair of sentences.

(5) When pages 3 and 4 have been worked through once, repeat them quickly using two pupils on each pair of sentences. Each pupil both reads his sentence aloud in Latin and translates it.

(6) Work through pages 5 and 6 similarly. These sentences are recorded on the tape, and should be used for further training in the reproduction of the sounds of Latin.

Language note

The concept of 'subject' and 'object' is difficult to define whether in logic or in linguistics. The ABV relationship is much more readily understood by experience than by definition; pupils already handle it intuitively within their native language. The purpose of Stage 2 is to introduce this experience in the context of Latin. The experience begins in this stage, but it may be some time before accurate recognition is securely established. The note in the pupil's text is very restrained and is thought likely to be sufficient for the time being for the majority of pupils under the age of thirteen.

Discussion with the class might be handled as follows:

Teacher: Let us take a pair of these sentences and look at the difference between them. Which pair shall we have?

Answer (for example): 'Caecilius est in atrio' and 'amicus Caecilium salutat'.

Teacher: (Write sentences on blackboard, ask for translation and write it underneath)
Caecilius appears in both sentences but there is a difference between the ways that he appears in the Latin. Can you point out the difference?

Answer: In one he is 'Caecilius'; in the other he is 'Caecilium'.

Teacher: Good. Both these Latin words mean Caecilius, but we should notice their different forms and give that difference a label. Let us call 'Caecilius' Form A and 'Caecilium' Form B. (Write the labels on the blackboard) Now look again at the sentence containing 'Caecilium' and notice how it is translated into English. This is a kind of English sentence that is already very familiar to you in everyday speaking and reading; and you now see the Latin sentence that corresponds to it. Let us look at some more sentences and notice their A and B forms.

Choose sentences showing Form B in -am and -em. Then ask the class to look at the note on page 7. If pupils observe and comment on the common factors in Form B and wish to group them, the teacher may usefully confirm that their grouping is a valid one and that it covers the majority of words when they are in Form B. If comments and questions are not raised, and very frequently they are not, the teacher should not take the initiative in doing so. For most pupils, what has been said so far is quite sufficient.

Older pupils, probably those beginning Latin at thirteen, may spontaneously ask for a fuller distinction between A and B, and in this case there may be value in using the terms 'subject' and 'object' respectively. They may perceive that the A–B relationship corresponds to what they know as subject–object in English or another foreign language. But it should always be remembered that these terms, when used by pupils, may be lacking in much conscious meaning, for the ideas behind them are difficult. To offer an over-simplified or partial analysis of what the terms mean should be avoided. At best it is unnecessary; at worst it may cause confusion and loss of confidence.

Reading passages

Content

The two stories continue to focus attention on the domestic life of Caecilius, but the first passage, 'mercator', makes contact with the larger world outside by bringing a merchant friend to the house. The stories try to give an impression both of character and of function. Caecilius is at work on his accounts in the tablinum; Grumio, a cheerful extrovert, prepares something special for dinner; the meal is accompanied by musical entertainment given by the 'ancilla'.

Method

The impact of these stories upon the class is much increased if they are read aloud by the teacher with care for the quality of the reading.

Good phrasing, dramatic interpretation, well controlled pace; all these will contribute to 'bringing the text to life'.

When guiding the class in their first exploration of meaning, teach them to use the 'words and phrases' as a pool of information to be consulted as required. New words should always be first seen in their context. Then ask leading questions about the sense of one, two or three sentences before a version is given. Follow up hints at character and attitude, revealed, for instance, in such sentences as 'Caecilius Grumionem vituperat' followed soon, however, by 'dominus coquum laudat'. After the first reading, *consolidation work is essential.* This may include:

(1) asking the class to re-read the whole passage by themselves, followed by a rendering by two or three pupils.

(2) the class reading the passage aloud together (in Latin), followed by a rapid check on their grasp of the lexis (do this by asking questions about the meaning of a word or phrase *in the context*).

(3) listening to the tape-recording, with the pamphlet open or closed.

Consolidation activities should always be undertaken and should be as varied as possible.

Of equal importance are the links between the stories and the paralinguistic section of the stage. The second story, in particular, 'coquus in triclinio cenat', will benefit from the use of this material and by showing a number of appropriate slides. The pupils must be helped to visualise the scene accurately, to know how it resembled and how it differed from a modern dinner party, to begin to think of the characters as people in a social setting and not just as names on a page. The paralinguistic section might usefully be read for homework before the story is taken in class. Use the slides to reinforce the subsequent discussion.

Manipulation exercises

Exercise	*Criterion of choice*	*Pattern rehearsed*	
1	sense	S ii	AQV
2	sense	S ii	ABV
3	A short passage for further reading or written translation.		

These exercises provide opportunity for both oral and written work; and the value of the individual written exercise should not be underestimated. It is the counterpoint to lively oral class work.

Paralinguistic

Content

As this is likely to produce a lot of questions from pupils, it is wise to equip oneself in advance with additional information. Paoli, *Rome— its People, Life and Customs*, chapters 2 and 6, and Balsdon, *Life and Leisure in Ancient Rome* (Bodley Head, 1969), chapter 1, will be relevant.

Note that the informal family meals 'ientaculum' (breakfast) and 'prandium' (lunch) were eaten either standing or sitting; reclining on one's elbow was a formality practised generally at dinner, especially if guests were present.

Suggested activities

(1) 'The times of meals and work during the Roman day were a little different from ours, being rather earlier.' Ask pupils to suggest some reasons for this.

(2) 'How did the Romans tell the time?'

(3) 'Imagine yourself as a small baker and "cliens" of Caecilius. Discuss what being a "cliens" means to you. Write a dialogue of a conversation between yourself and Caecilius at the morning "salutatio".'

(4) Show slides (nos. 15–20) which reveal the kind of decoration that Pompeians often painted on the wall of the triclinium. 'What do you think of the idea of paintings about food? What other parts of everyday life did the Romans put into pictures (slides 24, 43, 44)? What other subjects did they like to have in their murals?'

(5) Invite pupils to make a model of the triclinium. The walls may be decorated with a simple food motif. Make cardboard figures of the diners reclining on couches and the slaves bringing the dishes to table.

(6) Young pupils, perhaps girls especially, may like to dress up in togas and stolas and enact a scene in the triclinium.

Stage 3

Linguistic information

Previous input   *Examples*

sentence	S i	A = A	Metella est mater.
		A = Q	Clemens est in atrio.
sentence	S ii	AV	mercator respondet.
		ABV	Caecilius pecuniam numerat.
phrase	Q	X	in horto
		I	suaviter
morphology	noun	A/	canis, etc.
		B/	servum, etc.
		E/	horto, etc.
	verb	3/	cantat, etc.

New input   *Examples*

sentence	S ii	VA	respondet Pantagathus.
phrase	Q	X	ad portum
			prope navem
			e taberna
phrase	nominal	aA	magnus leo, multus sanguis
		bB	magnam clavam
morphology	noun	A/	-ax (Syphax)
			-es (Hercules)
			-ex (senex)

Note Suppression of A now occurs in the pattern, AV + QV, 'Caecilius surgit et e taberna exit'.

Model sentences

This stage, which consists mainly of consolidation work, has no model sentences. Notice, however, that several linguistic expansions occur within the stories. Details are shown in the linguistic information section above. Perhaps the most important of them is the addition of an adjective to the noun (aA, bB), thus producing a 'nominal phrase'. This is both a significant advance in itself and also leads towards several subsequent extensions of the noun, such as strings of co-ordinate nouns, nouns in apposition and nouns qualified by nouns or noun phrases.

Reading passages

Content

This group of stories takes the pupil outside the family circle and introduces him to the city and some of the varied people and occupations to be found in it. The first short piece therefore is set in the forum, the social and business centre of the town. It serves to introduce the three characters with whom the main stories of this stage are concerned.

Pantagathus, whose name indicates Greek origins, runs a barber's shop. Throughout history the barber's has been a centre of male gossip and in Pompeii must have been a place where news and rumour were freely exchanged. Romans at this time were generally clean shaven, and the normal custom was to visit the barber sometime during the morning, rather than shave at home. The poet who calls in to recite his 'scurrilous verse' is a reminder that literature was a more public activity in the classical world than today.

Celer paints murals on commission and represents the school of Campanian artists who, while reproducing Greek mythological subjects, often from Greek originals, were much more than hack copyists. Their sense of style and form and their rich use of colour gave real quality to Roman painting.

Syphax, an imaginary character like Celer and Pantagathus, is a wily Syrian who makes a living in the slave trade, bringing skilled as well as manual labourers to the Italian markets. The number of slaves resulting from military conquest had declined, and so there was a need for the services of men like Syphax; prices were correspondingly high.

These characters provide an opportunity to say something about the cosmopolitan nature of the empire, reflected in a typical way at Pompeii as a result of the town's historical growth—Samnite, Greek and Roman occupation—and of its trading contacts with east and west.

Method

Generally encourage a good pace and work on the fluency of pupils' reading aloud.

'pictor': In this passage 'ad'+Form B and 'e'+Form E are introduced. These and other Q phrases are meant to be handled as whole units and should not be broken down into parts. Pupils will initially remember them as complete phrases. Additional examples are given in the manipulation exercises.

'tonsor': Note the pattern VA, for example 'inquit Caecilius' and 'respondet Pantagathus'. This passage lends itself to group acting, after the first reading.

'venalicius': This passage is on the tape. The recording may form part of the consolidation activity and might be listened to with the pamphlets closed. The final sentence 'ancilla Metellam non delectat' may partially explain why many pupils see Metella as an unsympathetic character, jealous of the youthful and attractive Melissa. Note the sentence in the penultimate paragraph, 'Melissa cenam optimam coquit', which is frequently rendered as 'Melissa cooks dinner well'. The use of an adjective in an adverbial manner is common in Latin and should not be dismissed as quite wrong here. Ask for a rephrasing and guide class to the version—'cooks a very good dinner'. This may be done by asking 'What kind of dinner does Melissa cook?' Comprehension questions of this kind, which lead the pupil very close to the answer, are a valuable means of getting over a difficulty.

Manipulation exercises

Exercise	Criterion of choice	Pattern rehearsed	
1	sense	S ii	ABV
			AQV
2	sense	S ii	AQV
			ABQV
3	sense	S ii	ABV
			AQV

Paralinguistic

Content

The pupil's text and diagram provide an initial survey of the physical features and pattern of the town. This section offers a natural opportunity for showing and discussing a selection of slides that illustrate the streets, forum, theatre, amphitheatre etc. For younger pupils the discussion may be made more concrete by imagining Caecilius or Grumio showing a friend round the town. Reference should be made to the civic pride of the Pompeians, expressed in public buildings, statues and inscriptions and the civic deity 'Venus Pompeiana'. Build up gradually the picture of a community thriving on trade and industry but also lighthearted and given to the pursuit of pleasure. The teacher may also wish to give a further historical dimension by outlining the earlier period of the growth of the town. Some of the following data might be used.

The first inhabitants of the low hill near the mouth of the river Sarno were Oscans. Their occupation of the site and surrounding countryside dates back to the eighth or ninth century B.C. The site itself consisted of volcanic rock, the result of some prehistoric eruption of Vesuvius. Vesuvius was a peaceful, conical mountain covered with grass, small pine trees and, on its lower slopes, vineyards. Urban development proper began with the arrival of Greek merchant adventurers in the seventh century, who recognised the advantages of a site which dominated the approaches to the Sarno valley and the fertile Campanian plain just inland. By the sixth century the Greeks controlled the whole of the gulf of Naples with a series of towns and fortified hills including Cumae, Puteoli, Neapolis, down to the peninsula of Sorrento at the southern end of the bay. They also had a strong naval base at Misenum and occupied the islands of Ischia and Capri. This defensive system protected Greek interests against rival Phoenician traders and the Etruscans who had at this time swept down from Etruria and occupied much of Campania.

In the fifth century the population of Pompeii was further mixed when the Samnite tribes descended from the Apennine mountains, seized the coastal plain and imposed their own culture.

Thus, side by side with the Greek influences, revealed for example in the temple of Venus and the temple of Apollo, there grew up a

3-2

59

strong Italic tradition which continued down to the Roman period. Language, religion, civic institutions and forms of architecture were largely Samnitic; and the leading families, such as the Holconii, were descended from the Samnite aristocracy.

It was not until the third century that Roman power extended so far south, but after the final defeat of the Samnite tribes in 295 B.C. Pompeii became loosely attached to Rome as an ally. Direct intervention in the life of the town, however, really began with the Social War in the early part of the first century, when Pompeii joined the Samnite confederacy and tried to throw off the connection with Rome. But in 89 B.C. it fell, after a short siege, to Sulla's legions; and in 80 B.C. a colony of Roman troops and their families was installed. A new official name, Colonia Cernelia Veneria, was conferred upon it.

In accordance with the usual practice when a conquered city was organised as a 'colonia', the newcomers confiscated a large proportion of the land and property. They also took over the chief magistracies and established Latin as the official language. Inevitably there were disputes and the new families faced a good deal of hostility. Gradually, however, they intermarried with the older families and the bitterness waned. Pompeii was growing fast. The amphitheatre had been begun in 80 B.C. on the initiative of the duovirs Quintius Valgus and Marcus Porcius. Incidentally this is the oldest surviving Roman amphitheatre. The same two magistrates also built at their own expense the small theatre by the side of the large open-air theatre. This second theatre, which was covered, held about 1,000 spectators and was used as an odeum for musical recitals and for mimes. A second suite of public baths was built just north of the forum (Forum Baths) with separate accommodation for men and women. The town was developing into an ambitious and wealthy provincial society. The divisions healed and the older families began to take a part in public affairs once more.

Under the Emperor Augustus expansion and decoration of the city continued, much of it financed privately by wealthy individuals. The forum was paved with limestone slabs; the temple to Fortuna Augusta was built with extravagant use of marble by Marcus Tullius; the family of Holconii enlarged and renovated the open-air theatre, also with a generous use of marble; and the magnificent new palaestra, just west of the amphitheatre, was now developed. It is a square approximately 150 yards along each side, surrounded by porticos. In the centre was a large swimming-pool, around which was planted a double line of trees to provide cool and shade for athletes.

It was during this Augustan period that an aqueduct, sixty miles long, was constructed to bring water from the hills to a group of ten towns ranged round the bay, including Pompeii and Stabiae in the south and Misenum to the north. This revolutionised the water supply at Pompeii, which had previously relied on wells and the collection of rain water. Public fountains were put up on almost every street corner, a constant supply of running water was piped to the baths and the council sold to individual householders the right to tap the water conduits and lead pipes into their houses for domestic use.

This activity was rudely interrupted by the earthquake of A.D. 62 in which most public buildings and many private houses were severely damaged. But it is clear that life went on vigorously. Private dwellings were repaired and reached new heights of sumptuousness, the amphitheatre and other public buildings were restored and a new and very large set of public baths (the Central Baths) was begun. Other buildings, however, such as the Temple of Venus and the Temple of Jupiter were still in a very damaged condition when the final disaster of A.D. 79 brought the life of Pompeii dramatically to its end.

Suggested activities

(1) The information in the pupil's text needs to be related to the relevant slides. After the text and diagrams have been studied, show slides and help pupils to identify the main features and structures of the town. Emphasis should be placed not only on their location but also on their social function.

(2) The growth of Pompeii was arrested before the development of blocks of flats (insulae), which were a feature of Rome and other large towns, but there were a number of two-storey dwellings, where poor people lived in small rooms over the shops. They also often lived just at the back of the shop premises and places of work. Discuss with pupils something of the contrast in housing conditions and personal

61

affluence. (See the chapter by M. Frederiksen, 'Towns and Houses', in *Roman Civilisation*, ed. Balsdon, Penguin Books, 1969.)

(3) Discuss the amenities of life in Pompeii. 'Where were the open places for meeting and walking? What entertainments were available? How did people get about? How did they light their homes at night? What did they cook with? How was news communicated? How did people know where other people lived? How did they keep cool in the heat of the summer and warm in the winter?'

(4) Duplicate an outline plan of the town and ask pupils to mark in the forum, the theatres, the amphitheatre, the large palaestra, the Forum and Stabian baths, the house of Caecilius, the sea-gates, the main shopping area, and name some of the gates. This plan could be worked on over a period of time with the addition of new features which are mentioned in later discussion or which are discovered by pupils in books of reference.

Stage 4

Linguistic information

Previous input			*Examples*
sentence	S i	A = A	Caecilius est pater.
		A = Q	pater est in tablino.
sentence	S ii	AV	filius bibit.
		VA	inquit Caecilius.
		ABV	poeta tabernam intrat.
		plus Q	
phrase	Q	X, I	in culina, intente
phrase	nominal	aA	multus sanguis
		bB	magnam clavam
morphology	noun	A/	leo, etc.
		B/	mercatorem, etc.
		E/	foro, etc.
	verb	3/	revenit, etc.

New input			*Examples*
sentence	S i	A = A?	quis es tu?
		Q = A?	ubi est anulus?
sentence	S ii	BAV?	quid tu habes?
		ABV?	tu anulum habes?
morphology	noun	A/	ego, tu
		B/	quid?
		E/	-e (in urbe)
	verb	1/	-o (tondeo, pingo)
			sum
		2/	-s (habes, quaeris)
			es

Note Examples of previous linguistic input will not be given after
this stage. It will be recorded by notation only. Examples of new
input will continue to be given.

Model sentences

Content

Familiar characters now begin to speak in the first person. They say what they are, e.g. 'ego sum coquus' and what they are doing, e.g. 'ego cenam coquo'. They also answer the questions 'quid?' and 'quis?'

Aim

Expansion of the verb to include first and second persons singular; introduction of questions.

Method

The advance made here presents few, if any, difficulties. 'ego', 'tu', 'quis?' and 'quid?' are the only new lexical items in the model sentences; the content of the pictures gives strong clues to the sense and pupils usually require little assistance. You might begin by reading Grumio's statements at the top of the first page; then ask the class to say what they mean, perhaps prompted as follows: 'Grumio is speaking. What does he say he is doing?' If necessary, the teacher can act Grumio's statements with due emphasis on 'ego'. Then give the other parts to individuals or to groups of pupils, having each pair of sentences read aloud in Latin and translated. Guide pupils to treat these first person statements and second person questions as being concerned with the immediate present, not with habitual action, thus 'quid tu facis?' as 'What are you doing?' rather than 'What do you do?'

Note

'ego' and 'tu' have been inserted with the verb as a pedagogic device to reduce the contrast between Latin and English at this point. They are gradually phased out over the succeeding stages. They should be treated initially as they are in English, i.e. as markers of the person of the verb; close attention need not be given now to the morphology of the verb itself, though this should be noted briefly. Experience of the morphology within the stories and the manipulation exercises will normally provide sufficient practice.

Reading passages

Content

The theme of the two stories, 'Hermogenes' and 'in basilica', is that Hermogenes, a Greek merchant, has borrowed money from Caecilius, but refuses to pay it back. Caecilius therefore takes him to court. Care should be taken to help the class with the conceptual difficulty involved in the phrases 'ceram habeo', 'anulum habeo', 'anulus signum habet', 'signum in cera imprimo'. You may need to explain the purpose of a signet ring. Hermogenes stamps the raised image of his ring on the wax tablet as an acknowledgement of receipt and Caecilius keeps the stamped tablet as proof of the transaction.

Method

Both stories introduce the first and second persons of the verb in conversation, where they most naturally occur. A good way to handle the passages is to ask pupils to take the parts of the characters.

'Hermogenes' needs three people—the narrator, Hermogenes himself and Caecilius. This passage is also recorded on the tape.

'in basilica' needs five people—a narrator for the first sentence, a magistrate, Caecilius, Hermogenes, an amicus. Once the sense of the passage has been worked out, more can be done with its dramatic form. The class can be divided into groups and the scene re-enacted in Latin. With a less able class the teacher may find it useful to have the incident interpreted dramatically in English before having it acted in Latin. Generally speaking, pupils should be allowed to read out their parts from the pamphlets, but in some cases they will want to learn their parts and speak them from memory. Dramatic activity of this kind gives pupils a useful opportunity to discuss the characters of the people in the text.

After several groups have performed, there might be a special rendering by the best actors in the class with everyone else contributing to the court atmosphere. This final performance could be recorded on tape. (Note that such recording activity would need to be done on a tape other than the Latin Course tape; otherwise the Latin Course recording would be erased.)

65

Manipulation exercises

Exercise	Criterion of choice	Pattern rehearsed
1	sense	S i A = A
		S ii ABV, AQV
2		This contains all the linguistic features so far introduced. It would be useful to have this done as a written exercise so that the teacher can assess the progress of individuals.

Paralinguistic

Content

The forum—additional information.

The temple (1 on the plan), which dominated the north end of the forum and was flanked by two triumphal arches, was sacred to Jupiter, Juno and Minerva. It was the Capitol of Pompeii. Seriously damaged in A.D. 62, it had not been rebuilt by A.D. 79.

At the opposite end of the forum (4 on the plan) was a suite of three offices, occupied by the duoviri (the two senior magistrates), the aediles and the council (decuriones), together with their staff of clerks and junior officials. This was the municipal headquarters of the town. Just on the south-east corner, at the point where the strada dell'Abbondanza enters the forum, stood the Comitium. In this building the voting in the municipal elections took place.

At the other corner (3 on the plan) was the Basilica. In spite of its size it was roofed—the timbers being supported on twenty-eight brick columns surrounding the central nave. It was probably built before the Roman occupation of Pompeii, perhaps about 120 B.C. The Basilica served the double function of a courthouse and financial centre. In some ways it paralleled the modern Stock Exchange. At the western end stood a high platform with an elaborate pillared front. This was the Tribunal where the magistrates sat to hear the cases brought before them.

Immediately to the north was the temple of Apollo (2 on the plan), dating from the Greek period. The 'cella' was raised on a high 'podium' in the central courtyard. At the foot of the steps up to the cella stood the altar, and just to one side was a tall ornamental sundial, given and dedicated by the duoviri, L. Sepunius and M. Erennius. Here were worshipped Apollo and Diana, each represented by a bronze statue, facing one another across the courtyard.

On the outside wall of the temple enclosure, in the portico that bounded the west side of the forum, was a recess containing the official standard of weights and measures. This 'mensa ponderaria' (slide 42) had a series of cavities of different sizes cut out of the stone slab, in which a person could check that the quantity of grain or other foodstuffs he had bought conformed to the official Roman standard.

The next building on the left, as one moves north along the portico, was probably a public horreum; finally, near the north-west corner, were a large public lavatory and two underground vaults which are thought to have been the municipal treasury. These are not marked on the plan in the pupil's text.

The whole east side must have been an imposing sight. The reconstruction carried out in the Augustan period had swept away private houses which previously had lined this side and had replaced them with a series of public buildings. At the north-east corner was the Macellum (8), a large covered market with little shops both inside and outside its walls. The centre of the Macellum was an open courtyard. In it stood a small building with a domed roof and a water-tank. A room at the front of this structure was used for religious ceremonial and one at the back served as a fish market.

Immediately south of the Macellum was a building with a large apse (7). This is generally taken to have been the Temple of the City Lares, which was possibly built in expiation after the earthquake of A.D. 62. Next comes the Temple of Vespasian (6), dedicated to the cult of the Emperor. The Eumachia (5) formed the headquarters of the guild of the fullones (fullers, dyers, cleaners of cloth) and had been given to them by a wealthy priestess called Eumachia. According to the inscription over the entrance that opens on to the strada dell'Abbondanza, she dedicated her gift to Concordia Augusta and to Pietas. These abstract deities represented Augustus' wife, Livia.

As this guild was probably the largest business group in Pompeii and played a substantial part in local electoral politics, it may be useful to give here a short account of their activities.

No fewer than twenty-four electoral notices for the year A.D. 79 specifically mention a fuller. For example,

L. Ceium Secundum IIvirum iure dicundo Primus fullo rogat. (*C.I.L.* IV, 4120)

Primus the fuller supports L. C. Secundus for the office of duovir. and

Holconium Priscum IIvirum fullones universi rogant. (*C.I.L.* IV, 7164)

The guild of fullers backs Holconius Priscus for the duovirate.

The fullones were not themselves weavers or manufacturers of cloth. Their work began when they received the woollen cloth from the looms. First they had to wash it thoroughly to remove dirt and natural grease; this they did by treading the cloth in tubs of water and soda or other alkaline substances such as urine. Next it was treated with fuller's earth to take the cleaning a stage further, and then beaten with mallets to give the texture a finer grain. This was followed by more washing, brushing to bring up the nap and bleaching. Finally it was pressed in a large 'pressorium'. At this point the cloth was ready to go for sale—some of it probably whole-sale at the Eumachia, some retail to local customers. But the initial preparation of cloth was only part of the business of a 'fullonica'. The other part consisted of a cleaning service. In particular, the Roman toga was a large woollen garment, easily soiled and cumbersome to wash. Many citizens probably sent this garment to the fuller at fairly regular intervals. They were washed by treading in a tub, dried over a frame and finally pressed. Four pictures, found in a fullonica which had been set up in the peristyle of a large house in the via Mercurio, describe the process in some detail. The originals are in Naples Museum; reproductions are shown in several books, e.g. H. H. Tanzer, *The Common People of Pompeii* (Johns Hopkins Press, 1939).

The sale of food in the forum, as well as in the specialised market halls, is attested by pictures that have survived. Traders would set up small stalls there, sometimes no more than a little tray on legs, sometimes a structure like the stalls in modern markets with a canopy over the top. In the open space of the forum and in the porticos they sold fresh fruit and vegetables, poultry, cooked delicacies and drinks. A Pompeian could buy a snack almost wherever he happened to be, either by calling into one of the numerous 'cauponae' or simply from the street vendors. Not only wall-paintings and carbonised remains reveal the kind and variety of things eaten at Pompeii; the graffiti also add to our knowledge. The following items, for example, occur— some of them as labels on jars, others scribbled on walls: cerasa alba (white cherry), palmae (dates), triticum (wheat), hordeum (barley), perna (ham), botellum (sausage or black pudding), sinape (mustard), lac (milk, usually from goats or sheep). The most famous of Pompeian delicacies was undoubtedly 'garum', a potent fish sauce that came in several varieties. The best kind was made from the intestines of the scomber (Spanish mackerel) that was caught in large quantities off Nova Carthago. There, in Spanish factories, the intestines were salted in vats and stirred daily for several months. When it was ready, the liquid, now called 'garum', was drained off and shipped to such places as Pompeii where it was further refined into the final product, which was both tasty and rather expensive. The chief centre of this trade at Pompeii was the shop of A. Umbricius Scaurus.

Suggested activities

(1) In the discussion, after pupils have read the paralinguistic section, add further details as appropriate. This will help to develop the idea of Pompeii as a place vigorously alive and may start pupils off on their own research.

(2) 'Write a short account of a visit to the forum by Clemens to buy food or by Caecilius to negotiate a business deal at the Eumachia.' Encourage pupils to develop the character of Clemens or Caecilius as revealed by their bargaining activity.

(3) 'What kinds of evidence tell us about the food and drink of Pompeii?'

(4) 'Construct a frieze of the forum. Put the colonnades and buildings in the background. Remember the forum was a pedestrian precinct, and so there will be no carts and no transport animals.' Let groups or individuals contribute different sections. This could be a project lasting several weeks.

(5) Another group or class activity that has proved successful is the writing of a brochure about Pompeii on the lines of a modern town guidebook.

Stage 5

Linguistic information

Previous input

sentence	S i	A = A, A = Q; main variants—Q = A? A = A?
sentence	S ii	AV, ABV; main variants—VA, BAV? plus Q QABV?
phrase	Q	X, I
phrase	nominal	aA bB
morphology	noun	A/, B/, E/
	verb	1/, 2/, 3/

New input   Examples

phrase	Q	X (per) X (de)	per portam de monte
phrase	nominal	A × 2	Actius et Sorex feminae et puellae senes et iuvenes
morphology	noun	/A	-i (Pompeiani), -ae (agricolae) -es (actores)
		B/	me
	verb	/3	-nt (ambulant, contendunt) sunt

Note We have already expanded the nominal phrase by the addition of an adjective. In this stage a further important expansion occurs with the joining together of two nouns in Form A, thus producing the structure A × 2, e.g. 'Actius et Sorex' and 'feminae et puellae'.

Model sentences

Content

These are arranged in two sections. The first, on pages 2 and 3, depicts street scenes; the second, on pages 4 and 5, shows actors and spectators in the theatre. The street in the illustrations is a simplified version of the strada dell'Abbondanza at a point just east of the intersection with the via di Stabia. Nearby is the thermopolium (slide 35) and the shop with the wooden shutters (slide 33). The people hurrying along the street are going in the direction of the theatre which is approximately 200 yards away.

The theatre, which is the subject of this stage, is the large open-air one with a seating capacity of 5,000. The picture at the top of page 4 shows the canvas awning stretched across the auditorium by ropes and suspended from wooden poles set in sockets round the upper edge of the walls. The awning was usually coloured (see the paralinguistic section below).

Method

The new feature highlighted here is *plurality*. In this stage it is restricted to A (plural) + V (plural). The plural B Forms are postponed until Stage 8. The pictures provide easy clues to the meaning, and no difficulties should be encountered. The following are new items of lexis—puella, puer, spectator, actor, in scaena, femina, iuvenis—but in most cases they will be inferred from the pictures with a little prompting. One of the many ways of practising these sentences, after the first reading, is to ask one pupil to read the singular sentence in Latin and then either a group, or the whole class, to read aloud the corresponding plural.

Language note

The change from singular to plural is seen in the context of a whole sentence. The point that is being taught, though it does not necessarily have to be discussed, is that plurality is an aspect of both the Form A and the verb taken together. The contrast between, for example, 'servus' and 'servi', 'puella' and 'puellae' should be observed and commented on but not isolated from the context of the sentence. The terms 'singular' and 'plural' are introduced here.

71

Further examples

These may readily be devised by the teacher and worked through on the blackboard. Try to arrange them, however loosely, in a story sequence. Here are some suggestions:

1 puellae sunt in theatro.
2 iuvenes sunt in theatro.
3 senes sunt in theatro.
4 actores fabulam agunt.
5 spectatores in theatro dormiunt.
6 actores clamant.
7 iuvenes et puellae plaudunt.
8 senes non plaudunt; senes dormiunt.

Reading passages

Content

'actores in urbe' describes the effect of the arrival in Pompeii of two well-known actors, Actius and Sorex.

In 'Poppaea amicum exspectat', a quick-witted slave girl tries to pack her old master off to the theatre so that her boy-friend may call on her. He turns out to be Grumio, the cook from Caecilius' household.

Method

'actores in urbe': Because the lexical input is fairly high, it will be important to take the class through it carefully, before re-reading activities are attempted.

The excitement created by the arrival of the actors, who were probably 'pantomimi', may be compared with that caused by pop-idols today.

'Poppaea amicum exspectat': This should be handled as a play, after the first reading. The parts required are a narrator, Poppaea, Lucrio, amicus (alias Grumio), agricolae and iuvenes (the whole class or group). When discussing it and preparing for the dramatised reading, bring out the sense of excitement, the noise of people hurrying to the theatre, Poppaea's impatience, the irritation of

Lucrio whose sleep has been disturbed and his drowsy incomprehension of what is going on. Do this by questioning the pupils and encouraging them to make deductions from the text. This passage is on the tape.

Manipulation exercises

Exercise	Criterion of choice	Pattern rehearsed
1	sentence structure	S ii AV, AQV, ABV
2	sentence structure	S ii ABV, AQV
3	The passage rehearses S i and S ii in both singular and plural aspects. It may be set as a written test to assess individual progress.	

Paralinguistic

Content

In his account of images and reflections Lucretius describes in a most lively way the awnings spread over the theatre (*De rerum natura*, IV, 75–83):

> et vulgo faciunt id lutea russaque vela
> et ferrugina, cum magnis intenta theatris
> per malos vulgata trabesque trementia flutant.
> namque ibi consessum caveai subter et omnem
> scaenai speciem, patrum coetumque decorum
> inficiunt coguntque suo fluitare colore.
> et quanto circum mage sunt inclusa theatri
> moenia, tam magis haec intus perfusa lepore
> omnia corrident correpta luce diei.

This obviously happens with the yellow, red and rusty-coloured awnings, stretched over great theatres, flapping and fluttering from masts and wooden beams. The canvas tinges the assembly below and paints with its own colours the whole fine scene on the stage and the noble company of elders. The more closed in the theatre is and the more subdued the light, the more everything inside glows with beautiful reflected colour.

The scene is animated and gay. The theatre was an established feature of life in the Republic, and on its stage the comedies of Plautus and Terence and some of the old Roman tragedies were regularly performed. Under the Empire its popularity increased still further and every town of any substance had a theatre. But the quality of the entertainment changed as public taste declined. The writing of serious drama for the stage seems to have ended in republican times, and although Plautine comedies were occasionally revived, the most popular performances were of pantomime, mime and farce.

The theme of pantomimes was generally drawn from classical tragedy, but the mood was quite different. The appeal was more to the senses than to deep emotion, the chief attraction being the expressive dancing of the star performer (the pantomimus) accompanied by the rhythmic beat of an orchestra. The old fabulae Atellanae, with their rustic style and grotesque characters, were also popular in the first century A.D. They represented the continuity of a long tradition, but gradually lost the literary character they had once possessed, and reverted to a semi-improvised and topical form. Mimes too enjoyed continued and even increasing favour, but had no literary merits whatever. Their themes were vulgar and their language even more so. Sex and violence were paraded with unabashed crudity; and eventually, when the Empire became Christian, performers of mime were excommunicated, perhaps largely because they responded to criticism with satirical parodies of the Sacraments. In the sixth century Justinian closed down the theatres altogether.

But, although the crowds who turned out in Pompeii to welcome such actors as Sorex and Actius did not expect or desire entertainment of great dramatic quality, it should be remembered that the small covered theatre or odeum was built during the Augustan period for more serious performances of music and recitations; and that it would attract support from the more educated elements of Pompeian society.

The photograph on page 15 is of a marble relief in the Naples Museum illustrating a scene from Greek New Comedy. On it appear some of the characters who later appeared in the comedies of Plautus and Terence. On the right—a drunken young man, supported by a slave and waving the ribbon he had worn at a party. The flute-girl has obviously been to the party as well. On the left—the angry father and his elderly friend who seems to be trying to calm him down.

Suggested activities

(1) Show slides (nos. 46–9) and get the class to discuss them with reference to the information contained in the pamphlet.

(2) Read to the class a scene from the *Mostellaria* in translation.

(3) Ask pupils to write a descriptive account of a visit to the large theatre at Pompeii.

(4) If the class has previously done a classical foundation course which has included some work on the Greek theatre, this may be referred to and a scene from a Greek tragedy be read to them—for example, Antigone confronting Creon in Sophocles' *Antigone*. Some simple discussion comparing tragedy with comedy might be particularly suitable for older pupils.

Stage 6

Linguistic information

Previous input

sentence	S i	A = A, A = Q; main variants—Q = A?
		A = A?
sentence	S ii	AV, ABV; main variants—VA, BAV?
		plus Q	QABV?
phrase	Q	X, I
phrase	nominal	aA, bB, A × 2
morphology	noun	A/A, B/, E/
	verb	present 1/, 2/, 3/3

New input			Examples
clause	ClQ	quod + S i	..., quod tu es avarus.
			coquus, quod erat laetus,...
		quod + S ii	..., quod Graecus agricolam vituperabat.
			..., quod sororem visitabat.
			..., quod intente laborabat.
		postquam + S ii	postquam Quintus atrium intravit,...
			postquam rem audivit,...
		ubi (where) + S i	..., ubi infans erat.
phrase	Q	X (cum)	cum agricola
phrase	nominal	B × 2	Caecilium et Metellam
morphology	verb	imperfect 3/3	scribebat, quaerebant, erat, erant
		perfect 3/3, forms with -v- only	festinavit, petivit, laudaverunt

76

Note (1) Expansion of the nominal phrase: this is now extended from A × 2 to B × 2, e.g. 'Caecilium et Metellam'.

(2) The composite symbol ClQ, introduced here, is used to denote a subordinate adverbial clause.

Model sentences

Content

Page 3, Grumio and Clemens are attacked in the street by a savage dog.

Page 4, Quintus saves the day.

Aim

To introduce two aspects of past time, the imperfect and the perfect tenses. The examples are limited to the third person singular and plural.

Method

The pupil's text has no specific indication that the time has been changed from present to past. A hint from the teacher may be enough; if not, point out the time change explicitly. The two past tenses are presented in a context which contrasts the situational aspect of the imperfect with the momentary aspect of the perfect. 'The slaves were walking' when 'the dog barked'. The interruption of a situation by an action or an event is natural in both Latin and English and is a characteristic use of these two tenses. But this distinction often causes pupils some difficulty when it is discussed, partly because languages differ in their treatment of aspect, and partly because English does not always formally distinguish the imperfect from the perfect. The periphrastic 'was -ing' is generally restricted to contexts with a marked emphasis on the situation; elsewhere we are just as likely to use the simple past form. Hence it is unnatural and misleading to require pupils always to equate the Latin imperfect with the periphrastic English equivalent; and this equation breaks down completely with the verbs 'to be' and 'to have'. It is therefore recommended that in handling these model sentences you should not analyse these two aspects of past time and should not suggest that the Latin imperfect must necessarily be given the English 'was -ing' equivalent. Use the context to guide the pupil to make the most appropriate choice of the English possibilities. The language note has been postponed to page 7, by which time pupils will be more ready to perceive the distinction of meaning, having inferred it at least partially from the model sentences and the first two stories. Older pupils may be expected to grasp the point more accurately and apply it more consistently than younger pupils.

The following items of lexis are new: timebat, superavit, pulsavit.

In this stage, the perfect tense has only the form in -v-. The morphology of the perfect is extended in the following stages.

Reading passages

In the stories, 'pugna', 'Felix' and 'Felix et fur', Clemens goes to the forum, observes a fight between a farmer and a Greek merchant, and then meets Felix in an inn. Felix, a former slave of Caecilius, is now a freedman. He goes, with Clemens, to call on the family of Caecilius and after dinner the story of how he gained his freedom is told.

Method

The short passage, 'pugna', contains simple statements of situation and rapid action in the past time. The use of the question and answer technique will enable the teacher indirectly to reinforce the difference between the imperfect and perfect tense, thus:

What was Clemens doing?
Where was he walking?
What did the farmer do to the Greek?
What were the Pompeians doing?

Some help will need to be given with the conjunctions 'quod' 'postquam' and, in the third story, with 'ubi' (=where). These are relatively colourless words and pupils' grasp of them builds up rather gradually. 'postquam' is for a time confused with 'post'. Experience is the only remedy.

Notice the moment of obvious emotion in 'Felix', when Felix first meets Quintus—'paene lacrimabat; sed ridebat'. Let the class comment and, if they wish, speculate briefly on the reasons for his feelings. The full explanation only emerges in the next story, and when reached should be referred back to this point.

'Felix et fur', after the first reading, should be dramatised. Let the parts of the thief and Felix be mimed. This passage is on the tape.

Manipulation exercises

Exercise	*Criterion of choice*	*Pattern rehearsed*

1   A passage of Latin with comprehension questions attached. The linguistic level of the story is the same as in the reading passages, and the teacher may therefore need to help the class through it. Pupils could be asked to turn to this passage again later and translate it by themselves.

2	sentence structures	S ii AQV, ABV
3	sentence structures	S ii AQV, ABV

Paralinguistic

Content

Further information will be found in Balsdon, *Life and Leisure*, chapter III, section 5, and Paoli, *Rome*, chapter 10. Slaves, freedmen and poor freemen would have worked together in many of the shops and business houses of Pompeii. Much valuable detail about these occupations is contained in Tanzer's *The Common People of Pompeii*. The purpose of the discussion in the pupil's pamphlet is to introduce, with sufficient detail, two features of Roman society, slavery and freedmen, which have no direct counterpart in present-day western society and which can easily be misunderstood. The condition and role of slaves in that society was complex; it differed in different places and times; it varied as between individual masters; it covered a range of experience from indulgent affection, respect and mutual confidence to distrust, resentment and extreme brutality. As an institution it needs to be explained in terms of actual Roman practice rather than by analogies with slavery in other societies, such as the southern states of America in the eighteenth and nineteenth centuries. Pupils generally find Clemens and Grumio sympathetic figures and are dismayed by the harsher realities of slave life, but, while it is un-necessary to dwell on brutality, the trend of discussion should be toward a balanced realism. The subject of slavery will be more fully represented in the pupil's text in Units II and III.

Suggested activities

(1) 'What kind of relationship does there seem to be between Caecilius and his slaves in the stories you have read so far? What sort of jobs did the slaves in his household perform? What other work was done by slaves in Pompeii?'

(2) 'What sort of difficulties would face a slave who was brought into Roman society as a young adult from a distant country?'

(3) 'What parts of Grumio's life as a slave would you find it hard to bear? What compensations would you find in it?'

(4) 'Write an imaginary letter from Felix shortly after gaining his freedom (*a*) to Caecilius and (*b*) to a fellow freedman. Think about the different points of view he might express in these two letters.'

Stage 7

Linguistic information

Previous input

sentence	S i	A = A, A = Q; main variants—Q = A?
		A = A?
sentence	S ii	AV, ABV; main variants—VA, BAV?
		plus Q QABV?
clause	ClQ	quod + S i (A = A, = A), + S ii (ABV, BV,
		BQV, QV)
		postquam + S ii (ABV, BV)
		ubi + S i (A =)
phrase	Q	X, I
phrase	nominal	aA, bB, A × 2, B × 2
morphology	noun	A/A, B/, E/
	verb	present 1/, 2/
		present, imperfect, perfect (-v-) 3/3

New input

			Examples
clause	ClQ	ubi + S ii	..., ubi Clemens stabat.
phrase	Q	X (ad + Bb)	ad villam tuam
		X (in + Ee)	in loco proprio
morphology	verb	perfect 3/3	-sit (discessit)
			-xit (dixit)
			-uit (evanuit)
			fecit, venit, etc.

Note The complexity of Q phrases is now increased by the addition of an adjective to the noun, e.g. 'in loco proprio'.

Model sentences

Content

Caecilius and a friend dine together. The sentences trace the outline of the episode from the friend's arrival, the meal and storytelling, to the friend's departure. The scene is set for a more elaborate treatment of the same theme in the main reading passages. Notice that the meal is the 'cena' which began in the late afternoon and was the main meal of the day. At this meal the formal etiquette of reclining on the couch while eating would normally be practised, especially if a guest were present. The several courses would be served at a leisurely pace and would be accompanied by wine-drinking, sociable conversation and, often, musical entertainment.

Aim

(1) To introduce further forms of the perfect tense.

(2) To show prominently the feature of suppression of the subject (Λ). Pupils have encountered this on a graduated scale of difficulty since Stage 3, and should now be fairly confident. In the following stages, while the incidence and context of suppression is still carefully controlled, it occurs increasingly.

Method

Lexical help will need to be given with these new items: poculum, inspexit, hausit, plausit, dixit, sermonem habebant, surrexerunt, discessit. Make as much use as possible of the pictures and the story outline to help pupils identify the meaning of these words. There may be some spontaneous comment about the new forms of the perfect (with -s-, -x-); if not, postpone discussion until after the third reading passage, 'post cenam', when the language note tabulates the forms and contrasts them with the imperfect. The scope of this tabulation is merely to draw attention consciously to those contrasting features which are prominent and which have to be distinguished for the purpose of understanding. In any summaries that may be compiled and put on the blackboard, this principle needs to be observed carefully. To attempt to make distinctions on the basis of conjugations is quite unnecessary and may be positively harmful, especially since the material has been designed on the assumption that this aspect of traditional analysis will be omitted in the early stages.

Reading passages

Content

'fabula mirabilis', 'Decens', 'post cenam': This group of stories is about werewolves, ghosts and things that go bump in the night. It will be helpful if the teacher sets the scene of mysterious happenings from the beginning, noting the absent guest. The atmosphere of mystery and the unexpected should be maintained through to the third passage, in order to assist the deliberate bathos of the cat incident. The Romans certainly seem to have been partial to stories of this kind and after dinner was probably a popular time for telling them. Belief in ghosts, as a manifestation of the spirit of a dead person, was widespread and was closely connected with popular views about the after-life and the shadowy existence of the dead. Hence the theme of the paralinguistic section of this stage.

Method

Reading with dramatic tension will be essential for presenting these stories effectively. 'Decens' is intended for dramatisation after the first reading. 'post cenam' is probably best handled not by translation at all, but by good reading aloud and plenty of comprehension questions. The point will be readily perceived. 'fabula mirabilis' and 'post cenam' are on the tape.

Manipulation exercises

Exercise	*Criterion of choice*	*Pattern rehearsed*
1	sentence structure concord of number	S ii AQV, ABV
2	translation of pairs of sentences The imperfect and perfect tenses are contrasted. Encourage pupils to render the tenses with normal English equivalents rather than adhere rigidly to the 'was -ing' form.	

Further reading passages

(It is important to do these two passages since they contain a linguistic advance in the perfect tense. See note below.)

Content

'venatio': Quintus is taken on a boar hunt by his friend Gaius, and distinguishes himself. Hunting was one of the regular sports of nobles and other well-to-do people; and their sons would be trained in the arts of riding and handling hunting-weapons as soon as they were old enough. See Balsdon, *Life and Leisure*, pp. 219–20 for reference to hunting, and pp. 159–61 for a discussion of the sporting and semi-military activities of the youth movement 'Iuventus' instituted by Augustus. A description of the techniques of hunting and fishing is given by Paoli, *Rome*, chapter 22.

In 'Metella et Melissa', which appeals more to girls, Metella finds Melissa in a tearful mood and wants to know why. She administers comfort and generally appears sympathetic; yet this story apparently has little effect on Metella's image in the eyes of many pupils, who usually see her as a rather hard and dominating figure. The passage is suitable for group drama.

Linguistic aim and method

At this point in the stage, forms of the perfect tense of the type 'cepit', 'fecit', 'respondit', are first introduced. They can be noted in passing or be left until the end of the stage, where they are gathered into a list on page 15. Comparison is made with their form in the present tense, since this is the point of greatest similarity and, inevitably, a source of some confusion for some pupils. Attention to pronunciation will be helpful in the case of several of these words and essential for 'venit' and 'vēnit'.

Paralinguistic

Content

For Roman superstitions see Paoli, *Rome*, chapter 26, and for superstitions particularly about dates see Balsdon, *Life and Leisure*, pp. 65–7.

For beliefs about life after death, funeral rites and wills see Paoli, chapter 11, and Balsdon, chapter III, section 8.

How strong a hold superstitition had on the Roman mind is difficult to say; it probably varied with different periods and, in particular, with educated and uneducated people. Some of the darker beliefs about malevolent spirits derive from Etruscan influence and may have survived chiefly as tales told to naughty children. The arrival of Greek and Oriental culture in Italy from the second century B.C. brought with it magic and mystical belief as well as philosophy, though belief in unlucky days, omens and the power of incantations goes back much further and again has its origin partly in Etruscan culture. In some form or other superstition is a universal characteristic of human behaviour and springs from a sense of the reality and power of the supernatural. On the question of life after death, it is helpful to keep in mind that the expectation of life in the Roman world was a good deal shorter than today and therefore death was a more familiar occurrence in the family. The Roman was regularly reminded of life's brevity and it would be natural for him to give attention to the customs and memorials by which he hoped to be remembered.

This topic may seem rather sombre and should not be pressed too far, partly because it will, in many cases, be remote from pupils' immediate experience or in occasional cases be too painfully close to it. But the subject is a part of reality and, if handled with care, may evoke very worthwhile discussion.

Suggested activities

(1) 'Why do you think that the excavation of ancient tombs is sometimes very helpful to the archaeologist?'

(2) 'What kind of notices and memorials do we use today for somebody who has died?'

(3) What sort of superstitions are believed or half-believed by the pupils themselves? Do they take them seriously?

(4) With older pupils it might be possible to consider whether the public ritualistic nature of Roman mourning would help to assuage personal grief.

Stage 8

Linguistic information

Previous input

sentence	S i	A = A, A = Q; main variants—Q = A? A = A?
sentence	S ii	AV, ABV; main variants—VA, BAV? plus Q QABV?
clause	ClQ	quod + S i, quod + S ii postquam + S ii ubi + S i, ubi + S ii
phrase	Q	X (including ad + Bb, in + Ee), I
phrase	nominal	aA, bB, A × 2, B × 2
morphology	noun	A/A, B/, E/
	verb	present 1/, 2/; imperfect 3/3; perfect 3/3 (all main forms)

New input

			Examples
morphology	noun	/B	-os (nuntios), -as (feminas), -es (gladiatores)

Model sentences

Content

A display of gladiators is announced and the people of Pompeii hurry to the amphitheatre to watch.

Aim

To introduce the plural Form B into the sentence pattern.

Method

The pictures should provide a sufficiently strong clue to the new feature of language. Comment may be left until the sentences have been gone through twice. The following lexical items are new: spectaculum, nuntiabant, gladiatores, clausae.

Language note

This reviews, with familiar examples, the build-up of the forms of the noun in Stage 2, Stage 5, and the present Stage 8. The lists are designed to point to one contrastive aspect at a time, not as a vertical paradigm. Thus list 1 contrasts singular A with singular B; list 2 contrasts singular A with plural A; list 3 contrasts singular B with plural B.

Reading passages

Content

The three stories, 'ad amphitheatrum', 'in arena', 'venatio', are closely related and are based on the riot which occurred at Pompeii in A.D. 59 between the Pompeians and the Nucerini. The historical events are reported by Tacitus in *Annals* xiv, 17.

Method

To help pupils to grasp the situation and events described in the Latin, it may be useful if they read through the paralinguistic section first. The sentences in all these stories tend to be rather long because they are giving intensive rehearsal of clauses introduced by 'quod', 'postquam', 'ubi'. The teacher should look out for signs of in-security arising from the fact of length or complexity. Give pupils a little longer to explore for themselves: let the questioning cover the sentence fully. It will also help pupils to observe clause boundaries if you read aloud with emphasis and appropriate pauses. Questions have been attached to 'venatio' so that it may be used mainly as a comprehension exercise. The last three questions should be taken in conjunction with the paralinguistic section and used as the starting point of a discussion.

'pastor et leo' is a revision piece which contains examples of most of the morphology introduced so far. Younger pupils enjoy acting this piece, usually on comic lines.

Note that here the personal markers 'ego' and 'tu' begin to be suppressed before verbs in the present tense. 'in arena' and 'venatio' are on the tape.

Manipulation exercises

Exercise	Criterion of choice	Pattern rehearsed
1	sense	S ii ABV
2	In this short translation exercise all the verbs are imperfect or perfect. Each sentence contains a subordinate clause and a plural Form B.	

Paralinguistic

Content

For additional information about gladiatorial games see Balsdon, *Life and Leisure*, chapter VIII, section 8; Paoli, *Rome*, chapter 23; M. Grant, *Gladiators* (Weidenfeld and Nicolson, 1967). Slides 50–4 illustrate the amphitheatre. The drawing on page 17 is based on a wall-painting found at Pompeii. It shows the whole structure; and at the back is the 'velum' attached to the town wall ready to be drawn forward. Probably the work of a local artist, the picture shows the riot in progress with groups fighting in the arena, on the seats, staircases and in the area outside. Under the trees in the foreground are the stalls of the pedlars who, with the permission of the aediles, traded there, probably selling refreshments at the time of shows. Another sketch, showing a gladiator descending a flight of steps and holding a palm of victory proudly above his head, may well refer to the same incident. Under it were scribbled the words 'Campani, victoria una cum Nucerinis peristis', 'Men of Campania, you died with the Nucerians in the same victory'.

The holding of games in the amphitheatre was announced by an official proclamation, 'edictum munerum edendorum', from the magistrate; this indicated the occasion that was being celebrated, the date of the performance, the name of the magistrate under whose auspices the games were to be given, and any additional attractions on offer. The word for a free public show of this kind was 'munus' and it appears in no fewer than forty Pompeian graffiti. The giver of the games was called 'munerarius' or 'editor'. In the graffiti we find record of M. Casellius Marcellus, aedilis bonus et munerarius magnus, and of C. Alleius Maius, princeps munerariorum. In view of the unlimited enthusiasm of the Pompeians and their neighbours for these shows, it may seem a little surprising that any additional inducement to attend should be offered, but at the end of the advertised programme there is often a mention of 'sine ulla dilatione', perhaps referring to the continuity of the programme without irritating pauses between combats; of 'vela erunt', a promise to draw the awnings; and best of all, of 'venatio et vela erunt'—an animal hunt as light relief, and awnings.

The show itself began in the afternoon with a procession of the troupe of gladiators. They marched into the amphitheatre and around the arena. The 'editor muneris' also walked in this procession. The number of fighters presented varied, but twenty pairs was a common figure. After saluting the editor and the spectators, the fighters withdrew to wait for the signal to begin, which was given by the 'tubicen' on a large curling horn. A typical notice containing the basic information is this one:

A. Suetti Certi aedilis familia gladiatoria pugnabit Pompeiis pridie Kal. Iunias. Venatio et vela erunt.

The troupe of gladiators owned by the aedile Aulus Suettius Certus will fight at Pompeii on 31 May. There will be an animal hunt and the awnings will be used.

Pupils' reaction to the content of this stage may range from bloodthirsty pleasure to repugnance and criticism. While they should be allowed scope to express all these attitudes, the teacher's first concern is to see the games as a social institution, which, whatever we may feel about it, played a fairly prominent role in the use of leisure. Then, it will be useful to pass to modern forms of popular entertainment which to some extent appeal to violence: bull-fighting, football, boxing, wrestling and other sports involving physical contact. This is not to register approval of 'taking life to make a holiday' but to establish a perspective and to recognise that violence often has a powerful fascination.

Suggested activities

(1) 'Imagine you are spending an afternoon at the amphitheatre with a friend who is blind; describe the events to him. He might, perhaps, be an ex-gladiator with a professional interest in the arena.'

(2) Some pupils may appreciate an opportunity to write short poems on topics arising from the amphitheatre. Unless they have had much experience of poetry-writing in their English lessons, it will be best to restrict them to eight lines or less, and encourage free verse rather than a strict rhyme-and-rhythm structure. Those who do not wish to write verse should be given a prose alternative, again with encouragement to convey the atmosphere.

(3) 'An incised sherd (now in the Leicester Museum) links the name of an actress with that of a gladiator: "Verecunda ludia [et] Lucius gladiator". Imagine the actress is trying to dissuade Lucius from continuing his career as a fighter, after he has received his "rudis". What might they have said to each other?'

(4) 'A pair of gladiators is waiting in the tunnel just before going out into the arena to fight. They have trained together and are personal friends. What might they say to each other?'

Stage 9

Linguistic information

Previous input

sentence	S i	A = A, A = Q; main variants—Q = A?
		A = A?
	S ii	AV, ABV; main variants—VA, BAV?
		QABV?
clause	ClQ	quod + S i, quod + S ii
		postquam + S ii
		ubi + S i, ubi + S ii
phrase	Q	X (including preposition + Bb and Ee), I
	nominal	Aa, Bb, A × 2, B × 2
morphology	noun	A/A, B/B, E/
	verb	present 1/, 2/, 3/3; imperfect 3/3; perfect 3/3

New input   ### Examples

sentence	S i	= CA	erant Pompeianis tres thermae.
	S ii	ACBV	mercator feminis togas ostendit.
		ACQBV	Metella Quinto mox togam splendidam elegit.
		ACBQV	servi mercatori togas celeriter tradiderunt.
phrase	nominal	Cc	athletis notissimis
morphology	noun	C/C	Quinto, athletae, mercatori, Pompeianis, spectatoribus
	verb	new perfect forms	dedit, tradidit

Note For the time being the position of Form C is stabilised as the *second* element in the sentence.

Model sentences

Content

Quintus celebrates his birthday. Three elements of this theme are presented:

(1) Quintus goes to the palaestra of the baths where he shows off his new discus to his friends and practises throwing it.
(2) Metella, accompanied by the slave-girl Melissa, goes to the forum in search of a present for Quintus. She buys a toga.
(3) Quintus throws a party for his friends, at which Melissa performs as a singer.

Aim

To introduce Form C into the pattern of S i and S ii. For example:

<blockquote>

S i   erat Quinto discus novus.

S ii   Metella filio donum quaerebat.

</blockquote>

Methods

The new pattern of S ii (ACBV) generally presents few difficulties, especially if the pictures are used to help establish the meaning. Simple question and answer about the pictures elicits understanding of the 'transaction' taking place and this is then readily perceived within the sentence.

The relationship expressed in the new pattern of S i (= CA), however, is not quite the same, and a slightly different method of approach is required. The teacher has to establish the idea of possession: the first example occurs with picture 4, 'erat Quinto discus novus'. To do this, it is often helpful to have the second sentence, 'Quintus amicis discum ostendit', translated first and then come back to the S i C, 'erat Quinto...'. The sequence thus runs:

Pupil: Quintus showed his friends the discus.
Teacher: What had he got?
Answer: He had a discus.
Teacher: Good. That tells you the meaning of the first sentence. Can you translate it now?

This is usually all that is needed to get the class to understand the idiom 'est + Form C' and the further examples in this and the following stages steadily reinforce it. Most pupils have much less difficulty with the new patterns introduced here than might be expected. The teacher will find that they sometimes render Form C in the context of S i as if it were a genitive, for example, 'erat statuae nasus fractus'—'the statue's nose was broken'. This is a minor distortion that need not cause concern, since it correctly conveys the total sense of possession. Simply say 'Yes, or "the statue had...".'

Reinforcement activities will be especially useful in Stage 9. Go over the model sentences till they are thoroughly grasped; let pupils draw pictures on the blackboard, illustrating particular sentences, for the rest of the class to identify. In this way, pupils will be able to recall the model sentences easily, and use them as a means of dealing with later difficulty in sentences of similar structure.

The following lexical items are new, though the pictures will explain many of them: diem natalem, discus novus, ostendit, statuam, percussit, nasus fractus, donum, togae splendidae.

Language note

The Form C is placed in the second position in the sentence for the time being while pupils are becoming familiar with its range of inflexion and meaning. This temporary stabilisation also helps to reduce any confusion that may arise from the identity of Form C inflexions with those of other Forms. The language note contrasts the new Form with A and B, but only in the context of sentences, so that the contrast is made in terms of both form and meaning. To isolate Form C at this stage from the sentence is not generally helpful; to categorise it on a declensional basis merely leads to unnecessary complications and confusion. Examples provide the only sure way to understanding. Thus after the language note has been studied, the class could work through some of the following examples on the blackboard:

S i 1 erat Caecilio coquus optimus.
     2 erat Grumioni barba splendida.
     3 erat servis dominus benignus.
     4 erant mercatori multae naves.
     5 erant gladiatoribus gladii longi.

93

S ii

1 Grumio Metellae cenam paravit.
2 Clemens iuveni vinum ferebat.
3 servi Quinto anulum dederunt.
4 Caecilius amicis pecuniam tradidit.
5 venalicius mercatoribus servum ostendit.

Reading passages

Content

'thermae', 'in palaestra', 'in taberna' combine the theme of Quintus' birthday and activities at the public baths.

Method

The new linguistic structures are represented only lightly in the first story, and much more intensively in the following passages.

To help pupils to understand the technical terms—apodyterium, caldarium etc.—and the general social content of the Latin, it would be useful to begin with a preliminary discussion of the paralinguistic section, where a ground plan of the Forum Baths is given together with a description of the way they were used. It is the Forum Baths which are the setting of the story in the text.

The comprehension questions attached to 'in palaestra' raise the subject of Milo's character. The teacher could give a lead by inviting the class to speculate about why a statue had been erected in his honour at the palaestra. There could have been an athletics match against the people of Nuceria and Milo might somehow have given the Pompeians victory in the last deciding event. Alternatively, he might also have been a skilful charioteer and have won a great victory at Rome, thus bringing renown to his own city. The idea to be explored is that of bringing honour to oneself and the community and the means by which the honour was expressed visibly in the Roman world. Bound up with this is the larger concept of status and its labyrinthine ramifications in social usage. In talking quite simply about Milo, pupils are adding a little more to the development of this concept, and are learning to look beyond the merely factual content of a passage of Latin.

Further reading passage

'ad thermas': Caecilius goes to the baths and observes an incident of attempted theft in the apodyterium. The passage contains most of the morphology and sentence patterns given so far, including the new ones introduced in this stage. It is suitable for acting. 'in palaestra' and 'ad thermas' are on the tape.

Manipulation exercises

Exercise	Criterion of choice	Pattern rehearsed
1	sense	S ii ACBV
2	sentence structure (concord of number)	S ii ACBV
3	translation	S i A = A, = CA S ii AQV
4	sense	S ii AQQV, BV ABQV, ACBV ABV

Paralinguistic

Content

For further references see Balsdon, *Life and Leisure*, chapter 1, section 2, pp. 26–32; Paoli, *Rome*, chapter 19; A. Maiuri, *Guide to Pompeii* (Italy, 1964), pp. 32–5. Project slides 55–9 illustrate the baths.

Among the many Greek influences exerted in Roman society from the beginning of the second century B.C. was the habit of taking exercise before eating a large meal. The Romans exercised in the early afternoon; they took part in gymnastic exercises, boxing, wrestling, fighting with wooden swords, and ball games. How energetic they were about it depended on age and personal inclination, but we probably need not assume that the exercise was the most serious part of the proceedings. The bath that followed was the thing.

Baths were built in growing numbers, both in Rome and in the Italian towns. In the time of Augustus, Rome had 170 public baths, and they continued to proliferate until by the end of the Empire it is said that the city had more than 900. At Pompeii there were three public baths. The oldest, dating from the second century B.C., stands at the junction of the via di Stabia and the strada dell'Abbondanza. It is divided into two sections, for men and women respectively. It underwent progressive modernisation until in its final form it was lavishly equipped and decorated, and had some of the finest examples known to us of Roman stucco decoration.

The Forum Baths are very well preserved in parts. They were built about 80 B.C. at the beginning of the period of Roman colonisation, and like the Stabian baths have separate accommodation for men and women. In the men's section the tepidarium still has the large brazier which was used to warm the room in the days before the Romans invented under-floor heating. In the men's caldarium, at the end opposite the bath, stands the 'labrum', a great bowl in which a jet of warm water rose from the centre for washing the hands and face. On the edge of the labrum are recorded the names of the donors, the duovirs Cn. Milissaeus Aper and M. Staius Rufus, who erected it at their own expense in A.D. 3. They also tell us how much it cost them—5,420 sesterces; an interesting example of normal Roman self-display.

The third suite of baths at Pompeii, known as the Central Baths, is situated at the crossroads of the via di Nola and the via di Stabia. They formed part of the public works programme after the earthquake of A.D. 62, and were designed on a grand scale with large airy well-lit rooms; but they were never finished.

The main hours of bathing were in the afternoon, but they were fairly flexible. If no separate accommodation was available for women, they generally used the baths in the morning; elderly people also seem to have bathed in the morning. Most baths in the Italian towns, and many also in Rome, were run as commercial enterprises by private individuals who hired the lease for a given period of time. The hirer 'conductor' would appoint a baths superintendent 'balneator' and charge an entrance fee, usually quite modest. An inscription records the advertisement of such a lease,

in praedis Iuliae Sp. F. Felicis locantur balneum venerium et nongentum tabernae, pergulae, cenacula, ex Idibus Aug. primis in Idus Aug. sextas, annos continuos quinque.

A five-year lease is offered from 13 August on the property of Julia Felix, daughter of Spurius, consisting of the high-class Venus Baths, shops, stalls and second-floor rooms.

The Roman brought his own gear to the baths—his flask of oil, his strigil, comb and towels. If he was rich, his slaves carried these things and attended him through the various stages of the bath. If he was poor, he carried them himself and in the baths did his own oiling and scraping. For those who could afford it the services of various skilled attendants were on hand, the 'unctor', 'depilator', possibly even a 'medicus'. Refreshments could be had in the snack bars, 'thermopolia', just outside the main bath building; they could also be bought from slaves who sold them inside.

The function of these establishments was certainly not limited to a concern for personal hygiene. Bathing is a pleasurable and relaxing physical activity; and the Romans enjoyed it all the more in the company of their fellows. The baths were an extremely popular and fashionable social meeting place. They were also regarded by some critics as an indication of social decadence on a par with extravagant dinner parties. Some certainly deserved a bad reputation, being little more than a cover for prostitution. But the majority provided a valuable means of public hygiene and the lively atmosphere of a social centre. Uninhibited delight in the pleasures of bathing, chatting with friends, the shouting of attendants and pedlars must have filled these barrel-vaulted rooms with echoing din and good-humoured excitement.

Suggested activities

(1) 'What would the Roman bring with him to the baths? Describe the activities in the different rooms. How did they differ from a modern swimming-pool?'

(2) 'How did the central-heating system work? What improvements could have been made to this system by modern technology?'

(3) 'Draw a plan of a set of Roman baths and label it. Add brief explanations of the labels.'

(4) 'Imagine that you are an attendant at a Roman bath and that you are describing your job to a friend, while having a drink with him in the evening at an inn.'

Stage 10

Linguistic information

Previous input

sentence	S i	A = A, A = Q, = CA; with variants
	S ii	AV, ABV, ACBV; with variants
clause	ClQ	quod + S i, + S ii; postquam + S ii
		ubi + S i, + S ii
phrase	Q	X (including preposition + Bb and Ee), I
	nominal	Aa, Bb, A × 2, B × 2, Cc
morphology	noun	A/A, B/B, C/C, E/
	verb	present 1/, 2/, 3/3; imperfect 3/3; perfect
		3/3 including strong perfects

New input

			Examples
phrase	nominal	C × 2	Quintus rhetori et amicis
			argumentum exposuit.
morphology	pronoun	/A	nos, vos
	verb	present	sumus, facimus, estis, pugnatis
		/1, /2	

Note Sentence structures with Form C are not yet included at clause level. For the time being they are represented only in main sentences.

Model sentences

Content

In very simple terms the sentences sketch a 'controversia' in a school of rhetoric on the respective achievements of the Greeks and the Romans.

Aim

To introduce the first and second persons plural of the present tense into the S i and S ii sentence patterns.

Method

The teacher needs to establish the situation of a school debate. Without revealing in advance the details of the argument, he should make it clear that one pupil puts forward claims about the merits of the Romans, while another advances the Greek case. The class will try to discover the claims and criticisms made on each side. The pictures contain a good deal of detail and it is helpful to discuss each picture for a few moments before tackling the caption underneath. A little assistance may be needed with 'nos' and 'vos' but as soon as their meaning has been established, the new morphology should present few if any difficulties.

The following items of lexis are new: architecti, pontes, aedificamus, fundos, sculptores, barbari, utiles.

Reading passages

Content

The first passage presents the 'controversia' in more elaborate and dramatic form. Quintus and his Greek friend Alexander both attend a school of rhetoric conducted by Theodorus. The rhetor holds his classes in the portico surrounding the large palaestra near the amphitheatre. On the day in question, Theodorus presents the theme for debate—'Graeci sunt meliores quam Romani'. Quintus presents the case for Roman superiority and earns loud applause from the other Pompeian students. Alexander replies and, in the opinion of the rhetor, wins the day. The arguments are presented in simple and fairly concrete terms, but the teacher should look out for difficulties arising from those words and phrases that are necessarily abstract, e.g. 'graves et honesti', 'cultus proprius', and especially 'Graeciores quam nos Graeci'.

The second passage, 'rixa', has few conceptual problems. It describes controversy of a more elementary kind. Quintus acts as peacemaker when a quarrel breaks out between Alexander's two younger brothers, and takes the occasion to score a debating point over Alexander. Alexander however has the last word.

Method

The absence of action in the first passage and the simplicity of the situation in the second should be balanced by a treatment that brings out the emotional elements and touches of wit. The verbal exchange is not just a school exercise on a well-worn theme. It raises old antagonisms with echoes in the history of Pompeii itself; it appeals to national and cultural pride. Help the class to perceive something both of the formality and of the feelings involved.

Take the second passage, 'rixa', at a brisk pace, bringing out the contrast between the petulance of the small boys and the more grown-up behaviour of the others. There is perhaps a touch of pomposity in Quintus.

The personal pronoun markers 'nos' and 'vos' will gradually be dropped, but as with 'ego' and 'tu', they should be treated as part of the verb for the time being.

'controversia' is on the tape.

Further reading passage

'anulus Aegyptius' deals with the familiar theme of a magic ring and the consequences of owning it. The passage contains a considerable number of sentences with Form C, and may be used to give further experience of this Form and to provide an early check on attainment. Note also that from now on word order in S i sentences becomes more flexible and 'est' is moved frequently to a final position, for example 'anulus antiquus est'. This relaxation of order, in regard to the verb 'to be', becomes normal in following stages.

When reading this story, it is often a good comprehension test to ask the class to say who has the ring at any one moment. Pupils enjoy solving this problem.

Manipulation exercises

Exercise	Criterion of choice	Pattern rehearsed
I	Sense. A completion exercise from a pool containing Form B + verb (/I).	S i A = A S ii AQBV, ACBV

2	Sense. A completion exercise from a pool containing Form A nouns in the plural.	S i A = A, = CA S ii ABV

Paralinguistic

Content

An extensive general account of Roman education is given by H. I. Marrou, *A History of Education in Antiquity* (Sheed and Ward, 2nd ed. 1956). See also E. B. Castle, *Ancient Education and Today* (Penguin Books, 1961). Shorter discussions are given in Paoli, *Rome*, chapter 15, and in Balsdon, *Life and Leisure*, chapter III, section 4.

No books were found in Pompeii, nor has any room or house been identified as that of a schoolmaster. But the presence of 17,000 graffiti on the walls of the town, some of them official notices, the majority casual scribbles or private announcements, and the evidence afforded by drawings (such as those of Pompeians reading the official notice-board in the forum), leaves no doubt that literacy was widespread. By implication, therefore, schoolmasters were active in the town. In the wealthier homes private tutors, probably Greek slaves, would be employed. We find alphabets scratched on the lower part of walls, sometimes forwards, sometimes backwards. One graffito lists the names of the days of the week. It would be reasonable to regard these as the work of children who went to school. Other graffiti record proverbs, such as this one,

moram si quaeres, sparge milium et collige.

If you want an excuse to waste time, scatter grain and pick it up. or lines of poetry, often rather misquoted, from Virgil, Ovid, Lucretius and others. Presumably these derive from memories of literature learned at school. We also find a considerable quantity of amatory verse, which again is probably based on poetry learned by heart in the classroom. For example,

scribenti mihi dictat Amor, monstratque Cupido,
at peream sine te si deus esse velim.

Many of the Pompeians who scribbled graffiti were not members of an educationally privileged upper class, or professional signwriters. They were just ordinary people. There are, however, questions that cannot be answered: what proportion of the population could read

101

and write? how many children went to school and for how long? did many girls attend school? how many slaves were literate? It cost money to send children to school, even to the 'litterator', the primary school teacher. It was not expensive, but it cost something. And even in such a prosperous community, there must have been some who could not or would not purchase literacy for their children, in spite of the example of others who did. While it cannot be said that education was restricted to the few in the first century A.D., it would be unwise to suggest that it was nearly universal. At Pompeii, at least, it seems to have been fairly common.

Stage 11

Linguistic information

Previous input

sentence	S i	A = A, A = Q, = CA; with variants
	S ii	AV, VA, ABV, ACBV; with variants
clause	ClQ	quod + S i, + S ii; postquam + S ii
		ubi + S i, + S ii
phrase	Q	X (including Bb, Ee), I
	nominal	Aa, Bb, A × 2, B × 2, Cc, C × 2
morphology	noun	A/A, B/B, C/C, E/
	verb	present 1/1, 2/2, 3/3; imperfect 3/3
		perfect 3/3

New input   Examples

sentence	S ii	ACV	nos Lucio favemus. Marcus Quarto dixit.
		ACQV	gens nostra Holconio semper favet.
		CV	mihi placet.
		VC?	placetne tibi?
clause	ClQ	quod	..., quod vos Holconio creditis.
		+ ACV	Note this incorporation of the new sentence pattern in the clause level with 'quod'.

Model sentences

Content

Local government elections are the theme of the sentences and of the whole stage. Groups of Pompeians—farmers, merchants, bakers, young men—express their views on the candidates they have chosen. Present to pupils the idea of groups of citizens, representing various interests and trade occupations, putting forward candidates who had

103

won their confidence. Although women did not have the vote, they took a keen interest in elections. For details of the offices to be filled and of the families who regularly hold office, see the paralinguistic section in the pupil's pamphlet and page 106 below.

Aim

To extend the use of Form C in the S ii pattern, and to consolidate the C structures previously introduced.

Method

Form C is presented here in two new contexts,

(1) with a verb of replying, 'mercatores agricolis respondent', and, in the reading passages, 'Marcus Quarto dixit'. Note that one example of the new usage occurs in Stage 10, in 'anulus Aegyptius'.

(2) with two new verbs, 'faveo' and 'credo'. Examples,

> nos Lucio favemus.
> nos athletae credimus.

In these new contexts it may be preferable generally to translate Form C with a preposition in English in order to avoid initial confusion with Form B; for example, 'We give our support *to* Lucius'. But, equally important, this should not be insisted upon as the only acceptable English equivalent. 'We support Lucius' is also idiomatic English and, if pupils offer this version, it should be accepted.

The following lexical items are new: candidatus, favemus, credimus, pistores.

Reading passages

Content

'Marcus et Quartus', 'Marcus est iratus': The two brothers disagree sharply about the best candidate. Marcus supports Afer on the grounds that he is a wealthy property owner, while Quartus favours Holconius because the family has held high office before and has a record of public service. It takes a signwriter, 'dealbator', to resolve their dispute. The picture of a dealbator working at night by the light of a lantern shows the actual inscriptions discovered on the wall of the house of Trebius Valens.

Method

Both stories are suitable for dramatic treatment after the first reading. The use of superlatives and imperatives adds to the atmosphere and they should be stressed appropriately.

Observe that in both these passages there is an idiomatic extension of the S ii pattern in the form of 'mihi placet' and 'tibi placet'. In those impersonal expressions Form C now stands in the first position. They are glossed in the 'words and phrases', but the teacher should encourage a variety of suitable translations: for example,

> placetne tibi?—does that suit you?
> > is that all right for you?
> > will that do for you?

The imperatives 'scribe' and 'erade' are not at present identified as such, and should be treated as lexical items.

Summary of Form C structures in those stories:
S i   est Holconio gens nobilis. (From Stage 9)
S ii   Quartus dealbatori decem denarios dedit. (From Stage 9)
S ii   Pompeiani Afro favent. (This stage)
       Sulla Quarto respondit. (This stage)
       placetne tibi? mihi placet. (This stage)

Further reading passages

A play in four scenes 'Lucius Spurius Pomponianus', 'prope amphitheatrum', 'in foro', 'ad portum'. Grumio tries to masquerade as a citizen with normal voting rights, but the consequences are contrary to his expectations. The knock-about character of these short dramatic pieces makes them popular for classroom acting. They also afford a general revision of the linguistic input so far, particularly of the present tense (all persons) and of Forms B and C. 'Lucius Spurius Pomponianus' is on the tape.

Manipulation exercises

Exercise	Criterion of choice	Pattern rehearsed
I	sense	S i = CA
2	sense	S i = CA
3	sense	S i = CA

Paralinguistic

Content

Local government in Pompeii was based on elective offices and the
competition was lively. The bureaucracy of the Empire, which later
had a crushing effect on local political life, had not yet depressed it
at Pompeii. Normally the central government in Rome did not
interfere in municipal affairs as long as they proceeded smoothly, but
the riot in A.D. 59, at the show given by Livineius Regulus, led not
only to his banishment and the suspension of gladiatorial displays for
ten years, but also to a temporary replacement of the local system of
government by a centrally appointed 'praefectus'.

The elections were held in March and there were four officers to
be elected, namely two duoviri and two aediles. The duoviri were
the senior magistrates, and administered justice, while the aediles
were responsible for streets, markets and public buildings. Interest-
ingly, the liveliest campaigning was for the aedileship, since election
to the duovirate followed more or less automatically after holding the
lower office. The council of decuriones was not elected but generally
filled up with former holders of the magistracies.

Having been successful at the polls in March, a magistrate took
office in July. Thus at the time of the eruption in A.D. 79 the duoviri,
M. Holconius Priscus and C. Cerrinus Vatia, had been in office for
just about a month and the town was still plastered with electoral
propaganda. Normally these graffiti, painted on stucco walls often by
professional 'dealbatores', would fade quickly, but in 79 the destruc-
tion occurred within six months of their being painted up and when
excavated many were still in good condition.

About fifty families shared public office at Pompeii. These were
necessarily drawn from the wealthy class in view of the Roman
tradition that such offices were honorary and carried with them an

obligation to spend generously on civic amenities. They financed performances in the theatre and amphitheatre, the erection of new buildings and the renovation of old ones. Civic patronage of this kind had been a deliberate part of Augustus' policy of reconstruction, and many towns in Italy as well as Rome itself benefited from it in terms both of material improvements and of civic pride. One of the families which had had a long and distinguished career in Pompeian government was that of the Holconii. They had been active in the Augustan programme, had renovated the large theatre, held repeated offices, tended to monopolise the priesthood of Augustus, and one of them, Holconius Priscus, was duovir in 79.

The people who recommended a candidate usually advertised themselves, as well as the candidate, in the propaganda. Sponsors were varied—trade guilds, influential individuals, groups of neighbours or people who lived in certain quarters of the town. The appeal was generally made not to a political policy, since scope for that was limited, but rather to character. The notice was usually expressed in simple formulae. Here are some further examples:

A. Vettium Firmum aed. o.v.f. Dign. est.
Caprasia cum Nymphio rog.

We urge you to make A. Vettius Firmus aedile. He is worthy.
Caprasia asks this with Nymphius.

(o.v.f. is an abbreviation of 'oramus vos faciatis'.)

Q.P.P. aed. o.v.f. rogant vicini.

'vicini' often appear as the sponsors.

Several urge sponsors or candidates to wake up and be more energetic,

Trebi, surge, fac Helvium Sabinum aed., dormis.

In one instance a candidate's policy is alluded to,

hic aerarium conservabit.

This candidate will watch the treasury.

Another good example represents the people who lived near the Porta Urbulana at the east end of town,

L. Ceium Secundum II vir o.v.f. d.r.p.
Urbulanenses rog.

(d.r.p. is an abbreviation of 'dignum re publica'.)

Other groups who gave their support to candidates were muliones (mule drivers), sagarii (cloak-cutters), saccarii (porters), fullones (fullers), piscicapi (fishermen) and many others.

Some of these graffiti appear to have been put up with humorous intentions and occasionally perhaps to discredit a candidate. A group of chess players, latrunculari, decided to support the campaign of Montanus on behalf of his patron Lucius Popidius. Elsewhere 'dormientes universi' back the unhappy Vatia. But politeness or bargaining is the general rule,

> Sabinu[m] aed. Procule fac et ille te faciet.

The notices put up by the skilled signwriters were intended to be seen clearly from a little distance. Their letters, painted in red, were often a foot high. Sometimes they are signed by the writer himself. We find 'scripsit Protogenes', 'scripsit Infantio', 'Scr. Infantio cum Floro et Fructo et Sabino hic et ubique'.

And finally, as one wit put it when he contemplated the number of graffiti on a wall,

> admiror, paries, te non cecidisse ruinis,
> qui tot scriptorum taedia sustineas.

Suggested activities

(1) Invite pupils to comment on the picture of electioneering given in this stage and help them to draw parallels and contrasts with local politics in their own town today. Who are their local councillors? How often are they elected? How do they canvass support? What does a councillor do? What does the mayor do?

(2) 'Why did the Pompeians write on walls? Why did they not use newspapers, circulars, posters?'

(3) Put some of the electoral graffiti on the blackboard and help the class to interpret them.

(4) 'Write and deliver an imaginary speech made by a candidate for the aedileship in the forum. Don't forget his promises.'

Stage 12

Linguistic information

Previous input

sentence	S i	A = A, A = Q, = CA; with variants
	S ii	AV, ACV, ABV, ACBV; with variants
clause	ClQ	quod + S i, + S ii
		postquam + S ii
		ubi + S i, + S ii
phrase	Q	X, I
	nominal	Aa, Bb, A × 2, B × 2, Cc, C × 2
morphology	noun	A/A, B/B, C/C, E/
	verb	present 1/1, 2/2, 3/3; imperfect 3/3
		perfect 3/3

New input

			Examples
clause	ClQ	postquam + CBV	Caecilius, postquam Clementi anulum suum tradidit, ...
morphology	noun	/E	-is (flammis, viis)
			-ibus (infantibus)
	verb	imperfect 1/1	-bam (quaerebam), -bamus (timebamus)
		2/2	-bas (agebas), -batis (timebatis)
		perfect 1/1	-i (sensi), -imus (vidimus)
		2/2	-isti (discessisti), -istis (egistis)

Note The new morphology (/E, flammis etc.) is as yet incorporated only in Q phrases, for example, 'in flammis', 'cum infantibus'.

Model sentences

Content

The citizens perceive the beginnings of the eruption. It occurred just after midday on 24 August A.D. 79. Pliny reports that earth tremors had been felt for several days before, but as these were a fairly common event in Campania no special significance was attached to them. No doubt memories were revived of the serious earthquake of seventeen years earlier, and a sense of unease had troubled people's minds. But now the shocks were sharper and accompanied by thunderous noise. A cloud rose from the summit of the mountain. Ash began to fall.

Aim

To introduce the first and second persons singular and plural of the imperfect and perfect tenses into the sentence patterns.

Method

As with the present tense the personal pronouns are used as markers initially, and then gradually erased. The new persons are introduced in a context similar to that in Stage 6, where the tenses are shown side by side. The imperfect states a continuous situation; the perfect indicates the intrusion or occurrence of an event.

Note that not all the first and second person forms of those tenses are represented in the sentences. Nor should pupils be expected to have a complete mastery of the forms by the end of the model sentences. The purpose of this part of the stage is merely to introduce them clearly.

The following lexical items are new: sonos, tremores, sensi, nubem, cinerem, flammas.

Reading passages

Content

'mons est iratus', 'ad urbem', 'ad villam', 'finis': These stories present a connected narrative of the chaos that ensued. The centre of interest is the behaviour and fate of Caecilius, his family and his friends.

110

Method

Some classes become so involved in the movement of events towards their climax that they read very quickly to find out what happens. On the first reading they should be allowed to do this. The teacher's task is merely to help to maintain the pace that they set. The story is everything. Discussion of behaviour and the general picture of fleeing families and falling buildings, and such questions as how many got away, where they went and so on, can wait for the second reading. Given the high level of interest that is usually aroused by this stage, the absorption of the new linguistic forms occurs with relative ease. All the stories in this stage are on the tape.

Manipulation exercises

None are given in this stage.

Paralinguistic

Content

The story of the final catastrophe and gradual rediscovery has been told in many places. The information in the pupil's pamphlet may be supplemented by reference to M. Brion, *Pompeii and Herculaneum*, A. Maiuri, *Pompeii* or his shorter *Guide to Pompeii*, Wheeler, *Pompeii and Herculaneum* (Spring Books, 1966), Paoli, *Rome*, chapter 12. But the best description of the events themselves was written by Pliny the Younger. One or both of his letters should be read in translation to the class (*Letters*, VI, nos 16 and 20). A modern translation is available in the Penguin Classics.

So ends Unit I. Perhaps inevitably anything that follows this finale will be felt as an anti-climax, but not all the characters who have become so familiar disappear from the Course. Pupils may wonder what happens to Quintus and Clemens, and certainly there is no sign of them in Stage 13. But there is not long to wait. Quintus reappears in Stage 14 and Clemens soon afterwards, in new parts of the Roman Empire.

Suggested activities

(1) Discuss with the class the evidence of the suddenness of the end of Pompeii. 'How do we know, apart from the fact of the eruption, that the city did not just fade out of existence gradually?'

(2) Discuss some of the important principles of archaeology as they would apply to a site such as Pompeii.

(3) Individual drawings or a class frieze might be made of the scene in the streets or in the forum during the eruption.

(4) Invite pupils in groups to prepare and tape-record the script of an imaginary B.B.C. reporter who happened to be on the spot at the time.

(5) Divide the class into small groups; each group dramatises and rehearses an episode from the eruption (not necessarily involving the family of Caecilius); each group then performs its episode to the rest of the class.

(6) Set short individual or group projects relating to Unit I as a whole. Encourage pupils to choose their own topic and to pursue lines of inquiry in reference books.

Appendix A Objectives of the Course and its Linguistic Design

The theoretical principles of this course derive largely from certain ideas in modern linguistics. Although not drawn exclusively from any one school of thought, these principles are based extensively on the concepts of structural and transformational linguistics; and, in so far as any one linguist has determined the underlying assumptions that we make about the nature of language, Noam Chomsky has been a major influence in our thinking.

The task of actually applying those concepts that seemed to us to be important and usable was by no means straightforward. What was needed was both a new description of the Latin language, and a set of principles for embodying such a description into the design of a pupils' course. Neither existed at the outset of the Project. We were, however, extremely fortunate in being able to secure the services of Dr J. B. Wilkins of Queen Mary College, London, and of Dr P. A. M. Seuren of the Department of Linguistics of Cambridge University. Dr Wilkins made recommendations on the basic orientation and arrangement of the Project teaching materials, and suggested devices for the control of input, and for the construction of a gradient of complexity, from Stage 1 through to Stage 24. Dr Seuren guided the Project through the transition from Stage 25 to original Latin. Although neither is in any way responsible for the way in which the advice has been applied in the final form of the teaching materials, they both contributed so largely that it is impossible to conceive that the end product could have been achieved without them.

What follows here is not a full discussion of the research background. That would be impracticable. It is rather a sketch of the main features, and its purpose is to delineate some at least of the reasons that led us to diverge somewhat widely from the conventional handling of Latin. For those who would like to look more fully into the subject of theoretical linguistics some suggestions for further reading are given in the Bibliography. They will find, as in the study of other aspects of human behaviour, not a single, fully articulated account, but a variety of differing emphases, a shifting conceptual

113

landscape and frequently an uncertain relationship between field-work investigation and theorising. This situation is not a matter for surprise. It is the normal condition of a science that is developing rapidly. Nor is it unreasonable to attempt to make use of this body of ideas and research while it is still incomplete and undergoing continuous refinement. Future advances will reveal what we might have done differently or better. These, together with the experience of teachers and pupils, will make for constructive criticism and provide the basis for subsequent revision. This course represents a conscious change of direction; it does not mean the end of development.

Traditional objectives

Latin teaching has often had in practice several rather separate aims. These include reading skill, the ability to translate from English into Latin, and, by no means least, a fairly detailed knowledge of the categories of formal grammar. One reason for the variety of aims is historical: they have figured in Latin courses and textbooks for a long time and are rooted in our tradition. Another reason why these varied aims have been largely accepted until recently has been that while we have to some extent recognised their disparity, it has been assumed that for the learner there was a close and valuable connection between them. True, most of them are not regarded as self-justifying aims. The formal study of paradigmatic grammar and rules of syntax is related to composition; and both of them are viewed as the necessary background to reading Latin. Reading is the primary goal, but the contribution of the other activities is, generally speaking, assumed in the majority of course books and 'O' level syllabuses. That teachers have increasingly questioned this connection in recent years and have asked for a new type of material which balances the ingredients differently is evidence of a growing awareness of the confusion embodied in the traditional approach.

The confusion is of at least two kinds. The first is between language competence on the one hand, which is largely acquired by experience and the formation of implicit rules, and on the other, abstract knowledge *about* the language and its formal system. Such knowledge does not relate with practical skill in a direct manner. To fail to distinguish between these two different things is a serious confusion. It leads to several faulty practices; for example, explaining a construction in syntax before it has been encountered in the context of a passage, or drilling pupils in the parts of a noun or a verb before they are seen functioning in a sentence. The assumption often is that the prior explanation will be sufficient to generate understanding and accurate recognition; and that the drilling of the grammatical system will lead to understanding when the parts of it are encountered separately in a sentence.

The second confusion is between the skills themselves—that is between the skill of composition and that of reading. It is assumed too readily that the former may be used to teach the latter. The assumption is faulty. The natural order is, first, the understanding of linguistic signs, whether spoken or written, and second, the generation of sentences. The practice of writing Latin may be justified on various grounds, namely, as strengthening pupils' grasp of grammar and syntax; as an exercise to stimulate appreciation of the greater skill of the original writer; as part of the training of a future teacher or scholar; as an activity which it is enjoyable to practise for its own sake; but all these considerations point to a role which comes after, not before, reading competence. To use generative exercises as a prior means to this end seems to us to be of very questionable value.

The point is not whether the linguistic activities involved in analysis and memorisation of grammar, in generating Latin and in reading it, are interrelated at all. They surely are. But the connections are not simple and direct. The activity in one is essentially very different from the activity in another. Therefore, to use one as a means to arrive at competence in another can create rather than reduce difficulties, particularly for the average pupil. Better, in our view, to specify reading competence as the sole linguistic objective and then consider what are the means that are likely to lead most directly and effectively to it.

The reading objective

The effective reading of literature is a skill. This skill lies on two planes. First, the reader requires linguistic competence in order to arrive at the meaning and second, he needs to appreciate the content and style of what he reads. Learning is necessary at both levels.

The formation of critical judgment can only begin when the pupil is sufficiently involved in the story to make a personal response to it and is thereby motivated to join in discussion. In its simplest form the teaching consists of comprehension questions about the situation and events described. Whether the passage is a piece of synthetic narrative, a poem of Catullus or a chapter in Tacitus, the first question to be considered is always 'What has the writer said?' A full answer contains more than a plain statement of actions and events; it should also contain perceptions of character, motive and mood. One proceeds to the further question, with all its subtle ramifications, 'How has the writer said it?' Finally comes the attempt to form a judgment about the quality of the writer's achievement. Is it trivial or serious? Trite or profound? Imitative or original? The Project's course seeks to give some basic teaching in this aspect of the art of reading as well as in purely linguistic proficiency. Naturally, in the early stages the effort is concentrated mainly upon grasping the content and upon quite simple evaluation of character and attitude; but over the latter part of the course, in Units IV and V, pupils and teachers are encouraged to attempt more detailed and penetrating work in this direction. One of the legitimate criticisms of much Latin teaching—at least up to 'O' level—is that it has pursued technical competence in language often at the expense of any serious attempt to develop literary and historical appreciation; and this imbalance may lie at the root of many pupils' boredom. The balance should be redressed.

Again, in specifying that reading should be the sole linguistic objective as far as 'O' level, we have been influenced by certain characteristics that distinguish Latin literature from that of modern languages. First, it is not an 'open' literature. Its extent is finite and it is not accompanied by the existence of the spoken word. The literature of a modern language, whether it is the literature of the newspaper, novel or play, is open in the sense that it is constantly subject to change and has a real relationship with the current spoken language. There is therefore a proper case for approaching the literature of a modern language by way of initial learning of the skills of listening, speaking and writing. An obvious continuity exists from the one to the other; although even here the practice of modern language teaching tends to develop these skills successively rather

116

than all at once. Classical Latin, however, exists by itself. If we wish to employ an oral method of approach, the spoken word has to be restored artificially. Its artificiality is evident and its helpfulness doubtful, especially if a more direct line of approach can be made.

Second, Latin literature, like Greek, Sanskrit and other classical writings, is strongly influenced by conscious artistic principles. It is not merely a written form of speech. There is obviously a scale of relationship between spoken and written Latin. Some of the prose of Cicero or Pliny, for example, probably lies fairly close to actual speech; at the other end of the scale will be found poetry such as the *Odes* of Horace or the elegiac couplets of Ovid, with their visible and sometimes quite severe disturbance of word order and phrase structure. Nevertheless, the whole range of this literature is dominated by conscious stylistic canons. To prepare the pupil for this and to enable him to appreciate something of its flavour is one of the particular tasks of a Latin course; and the most appropriate form of such preparation would seem to be guided experience of reading, on a graduated scale of linguistic complexity and stylistic range.

A further consideration is that the full range of Latin style is too wide to be encompassed in a course lasting three or four years. What is required is a selected corpus which is both valuable in itself and also sets reasonable limits to the range of language and style with which pupils are expected to become familiar. We have chosen Virgil, Tacitus, Pliny and Catullus, with the addition of some Ovid and Martial. If certain norms of stylistic homogeneity could be traced and defined, within the limits of this group of authors, they should be anticipated within the synthetic course material. But the differences between verse and prose are wide, even though certain general influences of the one on the other may be observed. Even prose authors, such as Tacitus and Pliny, who belong to the same period, probably have few close affinities of style. Their common ground is the literary Latin of the late republic and the first century of the empire, but for the most part they are distinct and individual in the way that they handle the linguistic resources available to them: that was part of their genius.

Nevertheless, the synthetic material must aim, as far as it can, at preparing the pupil for the particular authors to be read in the course; and to this end it should have some deliberate orientation of style and vocabulary. We have therefore adopted, in the first three units, a conscious bias toward the prose of the first century A.D.

Grammar and its function

The 'grammar' of a language—in this we include both its inflexional and syntactic character—may be described in a variety of ways. A pure or theoretical grammar will seek a description which accounts for all the possible sentences of a language in the fewest and most economical generalisations. It will be abstract and will often use a symbolic notation. We may call a description of this kind—G 1. For teaching purposes, however, we need a description which, while it derives its linguistic validity from G 1 and may use some of its descriptive devices, also accommodates the particular objectives of the course and the needs of the learner. This we may call—G 2. It will, for example, vary according to the particular skill being aimed at, writing or reading or speaking. It will provide for the learner's need of a starting point within the language and for a progressive incorporation of new features into his experience; and it will relate to the target corpus of literature. In these ways a G 2 grammar will be deliberately selective and not exhaustive in its treatment.

A third distinction also has to be considered. The primary purpose of the G 2 grammar is to establish the design principles of the course. It is not necessarily the grammar which will be presented to the pupil. Conventionally, even in the early stages of a Latin course, the learner is presented with the G 2 grammar in a more or less analytical form, e.g. the rules of concord in number and gender, the categories of nouns and verbs, statements about the syntactic functions of the case system, etc. The necessity, even the advisability, of this practice should however be questioned, since it tends to confuse knowledge about the language with competence in language. The latter is something personal to the pupil. He already knows, in a functional, largely unanalysed way, what the structural possibilities of his own language are and may also have had some experience of a modern foreign language. He will grasp the structural patterns of Latin by comparing them concretely with a range of English equivalents. He will acquire the inflexional system of Latin mainly through a process of familiarisation and hypothesis, a process which should begin by seeing the inflexions in the context of complete sentences. In this context they will be observed as what they really are, a subsystem of the language rather than a major structural system. Much of the learning in this crucial phase consists of the implicit formation of tentative rules, below the level of overt generalisations, and is validated by the growing bulk of experience. These hypotheses do not remain an amorphous mass of isolated insights. The pupil organises them in his own way. He may be helped by a few general propositions and a limited number of labels for categories, such as labels for the tenses of the verb and for the cases of the noun. But he will be helped most by comparing actual Latin sentences, properly selected and framed, with their English equivalents. These insights, provisionally organised by the pupil himself with a modicum of formal description, represent a further type of grammar: G 3. It is flexible and subject to progressive revision and elaboration. Some pupils who have an aptitude for analysis will gradually wish to convert it into an overtly expressed system; that is to say they will arrive at G 2. Many others, probably the majority, will do so only partially.

Opinion will, of course, vary about the extent to which the formation of an effective personal grammar requires the assistance of formal grammar, and to make decisions about this is one of the most difficult tasks that teachers and writers of language courses are called upon to make. Nevertheless, the observations of modern research and the consequent increase of our understanding of the rule-determined character of linguistic competence have made it clear beyond doubt that anyone who is proficient in a non-native language 'knows', in a largely unconscious, implicit way, very much more about the foreign language than he could possibly have been taught by formal, explicit methods. With this in mind the Project has restrained quite severely the amount and kind of formal grammatical propositions offered in the pupil's text and has placed on the teacher the responsibility of meeting the need for further formalisation. The handbooks that accompany the separate units of the Course suggest ways of doing this. The grammar pamphlets for pupils that accompany Units II and III are intended as reference books to enable pupils to see some parts of the system in summary form as they feel the need for it. They are largely retrospective and are not to be used as preliminaries for new learning.

Objectives and linguistic design

The sentence

The starting point of the analysis adopted here is the sentence. The complete sentence and its immediate context constitute the most important operational entity, both in theory and for the practical purpose of reading. It is the sentence in all its possible representations that the reader has to handle. But, though the number of possible sentences is virtually infinite, the description of their structure is certainly finite. We have chosen two basic sentence (S) structures:

          S i (equational)   Caecilius est argentarius.

                          Caecilius est in horto.

          S ii (operational)   Caecilius in horto ambulat.

Even these two are interrelated, but are treated as separate for our purposes.

These structures are developed systematically and at two levels. At 'surface' level they grow:

(*a*) by the incorporation of new structural items, e.g.

        S i   est Caecilio villa.   = CA

        S ii   Caecilius amicum salutat.   ABV

             Caecilius vehementer servum castigat. AQBV

(*b*) by the expansion of the phrase groups, e.g.

        S i   Caecilius est *argentarius callidus*. Aa

        S ii *Quintus et Alexander* ad rhetorem ibant. A × 2

(*c*) by the expansion of morphology, e.g.

           S ii senex *iuveni* respondit.

                Pompeiani *Holconio* favent.

                libertus *dixit*.

                cives *gladiatores laudabant*.

The structures also develop in terms of 'deep' grammar, in that underlying relationships between different surface structures are exploited and emphasised. For example, there is an underlying identity between:

          Quintus amicum habet.

          est Quinto amicus.

          Quinti amicus

The same proposition underlies:

          gladiator Decentem necavit.

          Decens a gladiatore necatus est.

Similarly the language has embedding properties, by which a whole sentence is embedded within another sentence, for example:

Nucerini amphitheatrum non habebant.

may become by transformation, e.g.

(i) Nucerini, quod amphitheatrum non habebant, saepe ad amphitheatrum Pompeianum veniebant.

(ii) Quintus negavit Nucerinos amphitheatrum habere.

Another type of embedding occurs when a sentence is transformed into a nominal phrase, for example:

spectatores clamabant.

may become

clamores spectatorum

To describe the grammatical relationship between simple statements and the variety of possible surface structures in which they may be expressed, modern grammar has developed this concept of 'transformation'. It defines the relationship in terms of rules, generally known as 'rewrite rules', which when applied in correct form and sequence generate the full range of normal sentences. Conventional Latin grammar does, in fact, recognise and describe many of the most obvious instances of transformation, e.g. the grammatical relationship between direct and indirect speech, but the conventional rules are often formulated incompletely, in that they generate too narrow a range of usage, or are confused because they apply semantic as well as grammatical criteria to the transformation.

Another characteristic of the language which is widespread and often used for deliberate effect is that of 'stringing' or accumulation. All parts of the sentence are capable of extension in this way— nominal phrases, qualifying phrases, clauses, and verbs—and sentences themselves are quite often co-ordinated. In itself a simple device, it can nevertheless add considerably to the difficulty of any given phrase or sentence. The Project material carefully controls the incidence and growth of this feature.

Language learning

Some of the main principles of learning a foreign language have been mentioned in the foregoing sections. They are summarised here and certain further points added.

121

First, reading Latin is a skill, whose acquisition is dependent more upon exposure and implicit rule formation than on the conscious learning of explicit rules. Pure immersion in unsimplified literary Latin will not, of course, succeed. Techniques based simply on an analogy of the way in which a child learns its native language are misconceived for several reasons. The kind of process through which the infant acquires the mother tongue can never be repeated, since we cannot recreate the original situation. The intense practical motivation and constant exposure to linguistic data that characterised the original learning cannot be repeated in the context of the classroom.

Therefore, the learning process has to be compressed, intensified, graded and adapted. Conventionally this is done by abstracting a grammatical system and sets of syntactical rules and by causing the pupil to learn and then apply them. Our experience suggests that greater efficiency may be gained by exposing the pupil to reading matter in which the linguistic structures have been organised on a continually rising gradient of complexity. The input of new features is arranged so that pupils may detect regularities and observe structural correspondences with his own language. In such a context, affording both intensive practice and implicit sign-posting, the role of formal analysis becomes that of an occasional aid or a concluding summary instead of being the principal line of attack.

Second, knowledge about the formal categories of grammar, including the traditional terminology, is less significant than the 'personal grammar' which the pupil uses in practice to arrive at the meaning of a passage. These are not entirely dissimilar systems but the differences are extensive. The former, G 2, makes distinctions by labelled categories, the latter, G 3, by the observation of contrasts that are functionally significant. G 2 will analyse the contrasts between English and Latin by the use of grammatical terms, G 3 by observation of concrete examples and extrapolation based on them. G 2 will be able to express, for example, the parts of the verb in a tabular sequence, whereas the pupil, relying more upon G 3, may not be able to produce the paradigms but will interpret verbal forms directly, from his knowledge of the language, not of the paradigms. More importantly, the personal grammar will make use of elements that do not necessarily fall within the scope of strictly formal grammar—the lexical meaning of words, the context surrounding any given sentence, the order of words. Above all, it is something that the pupil must construct, revise and modify for himself as he proceeds, otherwise his progress soon stops. The pupil naturally, and to a large extent subconsciously, endeavours to build up this working grammar. He does not see it as a separate or abstract entity. It is rather a performance mechanism, analogous with performance techniques in other fields.

Third, certain principles of design, which are now more fully understood than they used to be, have to be observed in order to facilitate the development of the personal grammar. They include:

(1) sufficient prominence to be given to new features on introduction. This may be done by model sentences with illustrations, by short paragraphs, by initially keeping down the complexity of the sentences in which the new feature occurs;

(2) sufficient reiteration not merely of the grammatical form itself but of the structures in which it functions. The Project material contains, embedded in its narrative, extensive recurrence of grammatical structures;

(3) variation of the context in which the patterns are encountered. To train pupils to extrapolate their knowledge from familiar situations it is necessary to present them with an extensive range of subject matter, and this involves not only the use of a fairly large vocabulary, but also much structural variation;

(4) comparison of the new language with the native language. The native language patterns are the strongest and in some cases the sole experience of language for the pupil. He will intuitively attempt to relate and interpret the structures of the new language in terms of his own language and inevitably some interference at points of structural divergence will take place. This interference is recognised as one of the largest obstacles in the way of the acquisition of any second or third language. It is often felt at points of sharp structural contrast and with idiomatic expressions for which there are no direct equivalents in the native language. On the other hand, teaching experience suggests that interference phenomena and learning difficulties do not always coincide with sharp structural or idiomatic contrasts. Confusion can occur where there is close similarity of rules and idioms. Too little is yet known about linguistic universals to

predict accurately where the pupil will stumble. One still has to rely in this matter largely on intuition and the practical knowledge gained from teaching pupils. For the primary purpose of understanding sentences it would seem a better policy to take advantage of the learner's natural tendencies and use deliberately the similarities between the languages, at least initially, rather than to stress the areas of maximum contrast, as for instance Waldo Sweet's Latin course does. Such opposition between the languages may be feasible for older learners, with one or more foreign languages already mastered, but for younger and less gifted pupils it may be an unnecessary and undesirable additional burden. Broadly speaking language teaching has to choose between emphasising oppositions or emphasising similarities in the surface structures. We have preferred in general to exploit similarities where they are reasonably available. These include:

(*a*) initial stabilisation of word order;

(*b*) initial expression of the subject;

(*c*) the initial use of pronouns as markers of the first and second persons of the verb;

(*d*) qualifying phrases (Q), which are first introduced in the preposition and noun form, before moving later to pure case usage;

(5) motivation. Language performance appears to be closely related to the degree of interest felt by the learner either in the skill itself or in the content of the language. The more involved he becomes in the story, the more readily he penetrates the meaning. The exact nature of this relationship between motivation and competence is not yet properly understood. That it exists and is important seems undeniable. The Project has tried to exploit it to the full as a principle of successful language learning. D. J. MORTON

Appendix B Pronunciation of Proper Nouns

Aegyptius (adj.)
Āfer
Alexander
Anthrāx
Caecilius
Celer
Cerberus
Clēmēns
Decēns
Diodōrus
Fēlīx
Gāius
Graecia
Graecus (adj.)
Grumiō
Herculēs
Hermogenēs

Holcōnius
Īsis
Iūcundus
Iūlius
Latīnus (adj.)
Lūcius
Lucriō
Marcellus
Marcus
Melissa
Metella
Milō
Neptūnus
Nūceria
Nūcerīnī
Pantagathus
Pompēiānus (adj.)

Pompōniānus
Poppaea
Priscus
Pugnāx
Quārtus
Quīntus
Rēgulus
Rōmānus (adj.)
Sceledrus
Sorex
Spurius
Sulla
Syphāx
Syrius (adj.)
Theodōrus
Thrasymachus
Tullius

Appendix C Attainment Tests

It is important to be clear about the purpose of these tests. They were originally designed to check the effectiveness of the Project's material during the classroom trials. It was hoped that the great majority of pupils would be able to tackle them successfully, as they contain structures which have been frequently rehearsed in the stages preceding the test. Generous lexical help was given, as it was felt that pupils should not have to struggle with unfamiliar lexis while trying to interpret sentence and phrase patterns.

The tests were not intended to discriminate sharply between able and less able pupils to produce 'a good scatter of marks'. A different set of tests would have to be devised for this purpose.

In the tests the words and phrases underlined are either new to the pupils or have occurred infrequently in the pamphlets. You may find it unnecessary to give your pupils all the words underlined, but it should be remembered that they cannot be expected to recognise words that they have met only once or twice before.

When you correct the scripts, we suggest the following points should be borne in mind.

(1) Any English translation that faithfully reflects the meaning of the Latin is acceptable. Structural equivalence should not be insisted upon.

(2) Lexical and morphological mistakes should not be heavily penalised when the pupils have not had long to become familiar with new words and endings.

(3) Pupils will probably have most difficulty with structures that show a strong contrast with English structures (e.g. suppression of the A form).

The great majority of pupils in the first experimental group found the tests well within their power. Where pupils have had difficulty, we have suggested that the teacher should refer them back to familiar sentences containing the difficult patterns (the model sentences are often suitable for this purpose), and then make up further examples for the pupil to translate.

Test 1

Please give this test to your pupils after Stage 4 has been completed.

ad carcerem

magistratus Hermogenem convincit.

'ego Hermogenem ad carcerem mitto', inquit magistratus.

'ego sum innocens', clamat Hermogenes.

'immo, tu es mercator scelestus!' respondet magistratus. 'tu multam pecuniam debes.'

servus mercatorem scelestum e basilica trahit. servus mercatorem ad carcerem ducit et ianuam pulsat. custos ianuam aperit. custos est Groma. Groma mercatorem statim agnoscit. Groma ridet.

'Hermogenes est amicus veterrimus', inquit Groma. 'Hermogenes villam non habet. Hermogenes in carcere habitat!'

servus ridet. Hermogenes tamen non ridet. Hermogenes Gromam vituperat. Groma est iratus. Groma mercatorem in carcerem trahit.

'cella tua est parata', inquit Groma.

Test 2a

Please give this test to your pupils during or at the end of Stage 8.

Metella et Quintus

Metella in atrio sedebat. Metella Quintum conspexit. Quintus e villa festinabat.

'quo tu festinas?' rogavit Metella.

'ego ad tabernam festino, ubi amici me exspectant', respondit iuvenis. Metella erat irata.

'tu semper ad tabernam contendis', clamavit Metella. 'tu numquam ad forum contendis, ubi pater laborat. tu semper vinum in taberna bibis. eheu! ego sum femina miserrima, quod ego filium pessimum habeo!'

'cur tu me vituperas?' inquit Quintus. 'amici mei cotidie vinum in taberna bibunt. nemo amicos vituperat. amici sunt fortunati. amici matres molestas non habent.'

Caecilius et Clemens, postquam e foro discesserunt, ad villam revenerunt. Caecilius, postquam strepitum audivit, dixit,

'eheu! Metella Quintum rursus vituperat. ego ad tabernam eo. in taberna vita est iucundior.'

Test 2*b*

Please give this test to your pupils at the end of Stage 8.

villa scelesta

in urbe erat villa pulchra. villa tamen erat vacua, quod umbra ibi habitabat. omnes cives umbram maxime timebant.

Athenodorus ad urbem venit et de umbra audivit. Athenodorus tamen umbras non timebat, quod erat philosophus. villam igitur emit.

postquam nox venit, Athenodorus in atrio sedebat. subito philosophus fragorem audivit. respexit et umbram horribilem vidit. umbra erat senex pallidus. umbra multas catenas gerebat. umbra, postquam ingemuit, ad hortum lente ambulabat. Athenodorus quoque ad hortum ambulavit. postquam Athenodorus hortum intravit, umbra subito evanuit.

postridie Athenodorus servos vocavit. servi palas portaverunt et hortum intraverunt. servi, postquam in horto paulisper foderunt, hominem mortuum invenerunt.

Athenodorus hominem rite sepelivit, quod philosophus erat benignus. Athenodorus umbram rursus non vidit.

Test 3*a*

Please give this test to your pupils during or at the end of Stage 12.

Caecilius et Phormio

olim mercator diem natalem celebrabat. mercator Caecilium ad cenam invitavit. Caecilius cum servo ad villam contendit, ubi mercator habitabat. servus erat Phormio. Caecilius, postquam villam intravit, multos amicos vidit. cena amicos valde delectavit. omnes multum vinum bibebant et multas fabulas narrabant. tandem e villa discesserunt. Caecilius et Phormio quoque discesserunt. viae erant desertae, quod omnes Pompeiani dormiebant.

tres fures tamen per vias errabant. fures, postquam Caecilium conspexerunt, dixerunt,

'ecce! Caecilius adest. Caecilius est argentarius. est Caecilio multa pecunia.'

fures Caecilium ferociter pulsabant. Caecilium ad terram coniecerunt. Phormio tamen ad fures se praecipitavit et omnes superavit.

Caecilius postquam convaluit, Phormionem liberavit. Caecilius Phormioni multam pecuniam dedit, quod fidus erat.

Test 3*b*

Please give this test to your pupils at the end of Stage 12.

Imperator Nero

olim Pompeiani certamen musicum habebant. cives cantori optimo magnum praemium offerebant. multi cantores ad urbem festinaverunt. imperator Nero de hoc certamine audivit, et ad urbem advenit. omnes Pompeiani ad theatrum contenderunt. Neronem avide exspectabant. tandem Nero cum multis militibus et cum centurionibus theatrum intravit. milites et centuriones inter spectatores stabant et eos terrebant.

cantor primus, postquam scaenam ascendit, optime cantavit, milites tamen eum vituperaverunt. cives igitur cantori non plauserunt, quod perterriti erant. Pompeiani aliis cantoribus non plauserunt, quod milites eis non plauserunt. tum Nero scaenam ascendit. centuriones signum militibus dederunt. milites, postquam signum viderunt, vehementer plauserunt. Nero diu cantabat. eheu! erat Neroni vox rauca. vox Pompeianos non delectabat, sed milites Neroni iterum atque iterum plauserunt. omnes clamabant,

'Nero est cantor optimus. Nero est victor.'

itaque cives Neroni praemium dederunt.

Bibliography

These are recommended mainly for use by the teacher. Some would also be suitable for pupils to refer to under the teacher's guidance.

Books about Pompeii and Herculaneum

Brion, M., *Pompeii and Herculaneum: the Glory and the Grief* (Elek Books, 1960).

Maiuri, A., *Pompeii* (Istituto Geografico de Agostini, 1960).

Guide to Pompeii (Libreria dello Stato, Italy, 1964).

Tanzer, H. H., *The Common People of Pompeii* (Johns Hopkins Press, 1939).

Wheeler, Sir Mortimer, *Introduction to Pompeii and Herculaneum* (Famous Cities of the World Series, Spring Books, 1966).

Some general books

Allen, W. S., *Vox Latina* (Cambridge University Press, 1965).

Balsdon, J. P. V. D., *Life and Leisure in Ancient Rome* (Bodley Head, 1969).

(ed.), *Roman Civilization* (Penguin Books, 1969).

Barrow, R. H., *The Romans* (Penguin Books, 1949).

Carcopino, J., *Daily Life in Ancient Rome* (Penguin Books, 1956; USA: Yale University Press).

Crook, J. A., *Law and Life of Rome* (Thames and Hudson, 1967; USA: Cornell University Press).

Lewis, N. and Reinhold, M., *Roman Civilization. Sourcebook 1: The Republic*; *Sourcebook 2: The Empire* (Harper Torchbooks, Harper and Row, 1966).

Paoli, E., *Rome—its People, Life and Customs* (Longmans, 1963; USA: McKay).

Wheeler, Sir Mortimer, *Roman Art and Architecture* (Thames and Hudson, 1964; USA: Praeger).

Linguistics

Crothers, E. and Suppes, P., *Experiments in Second-language Learning*, see chapter 1 (Academic Press, 1967).

Halliday, M. A. K., McIntosh, A. and Strevens, P., *The Linguistic Sciences and Language Teaching* (Longmans, 1964; USA: Indiana University Press, 1965).

Lenneberg, E. H., 'The natural history of language', pp. 219–52 in F. Smith and G. A. Miller (eds.), *The Genesis of Language* (M.I.T. Press, 1966).

Lester, M. (ed.), *Readings in Applied Transformational Grammar* (Holt, Rinehart and Winston, 1970).

Lyons, J., *Introduction to Theoretical Linguistics* (Cambridge University Press, 1968).

Newmark, L. and Reibel, D. A., 'Necessity and sufficiency in language learning', in *International Review of Applied Linguistics* (May 1968).

Oldfield, R. C. and Marshall, J. C. (eds.), *Language.* See especially D. McNeill, 'The creation of language', pp. 21–31; G. A. Miller, 'Some preliminaries to psycholinguistics' (Penguin Modern Psychology, 1968).

Rosenbaum, P. S., 'On the role of linguistics in the teaching of English', pp. 467–81, in D. A. Reibel and S. A. Schane (eds.), *Modern Studies in English* (Prentice-Hall, 1969).